M W
& R

WHAT TO
LISTEN FOR IN
BEETHOVEN

WHAT TO
LISTEN FOR IN
BEETHOVEN

The Essential Introduction to the World's
Foremost Composer and to the
Hidden Pleasures of Classical Music

ROBERT HARRIS

Macfarlane Walter & Ross
Toronto, Buffalo

Macfarlane Walter & Ross
37A Hazelton Avenue
Toronto, Canada M5R 2E3

Distributed in Canada by
General Distribution Services Inc.
30 Lesmill Road
Toronto, Canada M3B 2T6
Tel (416) 445-3333
Fax (416) 445-5967
e-mail Customer.Service@ccmailgw.genpub.com

Distributed in the United States by
General Distribution Services Inc.
85 River Rock Drive, Suite 202
Buffalo, New York 14207
Toll free 1-800-805-1083
Fax (416) 445-5967
e-mail Customer.Service@ccmailgw.genpub.com

Cataloguing in Publication Data

Harris, Robert, 1948-
    What to listen for in Beethoven

Includes bibliographical references and index.
ISBN 1-55199-001-6

1. Beethoven, Ludwig van, 1770-1827
2. Composers – Austria – Biography.   I. Title.

ML410.B4H31   1996   780'.92   C96-931827-8

The publisher gratefully acknowledges the support of the Canada Council and the Ontario Arts Council

Printed and bound in Canada

To Dory, with love and hope

Contents

Introduction

"Without music, life would be a mistake," said Friedrich Nietzsche, summarizing a sentiment central to Western civilization since the Greeks. For thousands of years, people the world over have seen music as one of life's treasures. But if music — especially classical music — is a treasure, for many of us it is buried treasure. Buried in clear sight, one might add, the most insidious form of disguise.

It's not that the music is inaccessible. A flip through the radio dial of just about any city in the world will find you at least one station devoted to classical music. Even the smallest record store has its classical collection, some of them numbering in the thousands of CDs. The music is hardly hidden. But its appreciation remains a secret, guarded by silent overseers. If you want to find the musical treasure for yourself, it would help if you had a map.

This book is intended to be your map. It hopes to lead you to some of the greatest music ever written and to provide you with the tools to "dig" it for yourself. Classical music isn't that difficult to appreciate. You just need to know a little bit about how it's put together and how to pick out its distinctive characteristics. Classical music is different from pop music, but the two are not rivals. It is not a question of appreciating one or the other. Your musical world can include both.

This book is also a record of one of the towering artistic personalities of all time. Beethoven was the first musician who refused to separate his personal and musical lives. He virtually invented the notion that music could and should be a record of a composer's inner feelings and emotions. Coming into contact with Beethoven's music brings you face to face with his tortured and dramatic personality. The story of the man and the story of his music go hand in hand. To understand one is to understand the other.

No writer works alone. Once again, I am indebted to Jan Walter of Macfarlane Walter & Ross for the support and encouragement she gave throughout this project. All authors should be graced with such publishers. Kathy Vanderlinden brought an expert and fastidious touch to the editing of the manuscript. My wife, Candace, my best companion, supplied the care and attention that made the work possible, even pleasurable. She made the trials of its composition bearable by sharing them so wholeheartedly.

The Colossus

Once in a very long while, the circumstances of an age and the personality of an individual come together to produce an artist whose work is so perfect a reflection of human nature and longing that time cannot erode nor fashion affect it. Michelangelo was such an artist; so was Shakespeare. Into their company one freely admits Ludwig van Beethoven.

Two hundred years after his tumultuous life and heroic artistic struggles, Beethoven remains the preeminent composer of Western classical music. Born in 1770, just as the forces of revolution and social change were to sweep away the last vestiges of feudal Europe, Beethoven captured in his music a spirit of excitement and conquering achievement that has remained fresh and attractive ever since.

Unless you count in a portion of his own lifetime (the decade 1812–22), Beethoven's music has never gone out of fashion, never been absent from classical concert halls. This is true of no other composer. Bach was completely forgotten for almost a century after his death, until he was rediscovered by Felix Mendelssohn in the 1830s. Mozart was represented by no more than half a dozen works for most of the nineteenth century, which found him vapid and empty. There have been times when Brahms was very popular, others when he was ignored. Schumann, Chopin, Wagner, Mahler, Bartok and countless others have suffered the same fate. Although acknowledged as musical masters, their music for long stretches of time languished on the back shelf of contemporary taste.

Not so Beethoven. Virtually from the moment it left his pen in his scrawled handwriting, Beethoven's music has been the touchstone against which all other Western music, and much other art, has been judged. Popular with the general musical public and professionals alike, Beethoven found a secret in musical art that allowed him to forge a link of communication between himself and his audiences so strong that it has spanned tastes, cultures and generations.

The facts of his life are simple to relate. He was born in 1770 in Bonn into a musical family. His father was a court singer; his grandfather, the Elector of Cologne's *Kapellmeister*, the court's leading musician. Beethoven showed musical promise early, enough to attract the attention of Bonn's wealthier families. At twenty-two, he journeyed to Vienna, where he would spend the rest of his life. He soon made a name for himself as a virtuoso pianist and budding composer. As early as age twenty-nine, he began to experience difficulty with his hearing, although he did not go completely deaf until he was about forty-five. He never married, although his name was linked romantically with those of several women. In both appearance and manner he was a notorious eccentric, whose deafness only accentuated his social isolation. He had a tremendously mercurial personality and a furious temper. Yet, despite his personal difficulties, he became Europe's most famous musician, producing the greatest music of his time, perhaps of all time.

Beethoven lived during perhaps the three or four most exciting decades in the history of the Western world. Both the French and the American Revolutions took place while he was still in his teens. He was a contemporary of men of the world like Napoleon, Robespierre, Danton, as well as George Washington, Thomas Jefferson and

Benjamin Franklin. He shared his lifetime with Wordsworth and Coleridge, Goethe, Jane Austen and Walter Scott. Byron, Shelley and Keats were contemporaries, as were Immanuel Kant, Hegel and Schopenhauer. He knew and was taught by Haydn and was robbed of Mozart only by the latter's untimely death. Into his manuscripts he placed this extraordinarily rich world of politics and philosophy and preserved it for us in its vibrant freshness. He witnessed and, indeed, participated in the birth of romantic art.

Beethoven was not just a bystander to the great events surrounding him. In his own field, he was equally revolutionary. Before Beethoven, music was entertainment and decoration. With him, music entered a new realm, that of speech and the personal musical statement. Beethoven put into music feelings and ideas that had previously been found only in poetry and drama, and did it entirely within the sphere of pure music, without the help of texts or librettos. The extra dimension of mystery that music had always possessed made these deeper sentiments all the more powerful in his hands. Indeed, almost entirely because of Beethoven's work, music was revalued in the early nineteenth century as the most sublime, most spiritual of all the arts, a status it kept for almost a hundred years. With all the force of a natural phenomenon, Beethoven's powerful musical legacy cannot be ignored. Like a volcano or hurricane, it demands a response.

Beethoven's music enters the realm of poetry, but the poetry is often about pain and difficulty. No composer, indeed few artists before our own era seemed to wrestle with their art as Beethoven did; in no artist is struggle and triumph so important an aesthetic principle. On both a personal and an artistic level, Beethoven is about overcoming adversity, reaching for a new world through work and effort.

In this aspect of his art, Beethoven is more than a single individual; he is a leading representative of his age. Beethoven and our modern world were born twins, conceived at the same time, nourished in the same atmosphere, imbued with the same ideas, subject to the same spiritual heights and depths. Beethoven was a child of the Enlightenment and the French Revolution, the intellectual and political celebration of liberation, of freedom from tyranny, that still lies at the heart of our intellectual and political life today. Beethoven was a Napoleon of sound out to liberate minds and spirits rather than constitutions and laws. As such, he is the celebrant par excellence of the individual: a composer who through his art makes us feel the power of our own ability to accomplish and develop in the world.

Beethoven was the first "artist" as we understand the term today, and one of the first to appropriate the historic role that artists were to adopt in the decades following him. He believed that artists were closer to spiritual truth than others and had a mission to spread that truth. With Beethoven, art became a force to rival both philosophy and religion.

With that background, it is no surprise that Beethoven, even within his own lifetime but certainly afterward, took on the dimensions of a mythic figure, a central icon in Western artistic history. Just to mention the name conjures up a mental portrait of a scowling, defiant creator, a "Titan wrestling with the Gods," as Wagner put it. And not just his music but his personal life as well became interpreted within this mythic mold. Beethoven was not the only deaf musician in history, but his tragic affliction assumed heroic proportions. He became a sort of Prometheus, the god destined to suffer forever for daring to bring enlightenment to humanity, the tormented angel whose pain became transformed into the beauty of his art.

These three faces of Beethoven — the musician of genius, the tormented creator and the representative of an age — can present quite a daunting barrier to a listener coming to the music of the composer for the first time. Even in his own time, Beethoven was as much feared as revered. Poor, shy Franz Schubert, who worshiped the ground Beethoven walked on, went night after night to the restaurant where Beethoven had his dinner and sat in a darkened corner, trying to build up the courage to speak to his hero. He never did. The two great romantic composers never met.

You needn't be as reluctant to greet Beethoven as was Schubert. The heroic images of Beethoven, however faithful they may be, don't tell the full story of the composer. Beethoven was a genius, but he was also a man, and in many respects a very humble man. His music is undeniably powerful, but it is also crafted according to principles and ideas that are yours to discover. In the end, we do both the man and the music a disservice to elevate them to impossible heights.

Let us keep another Beethoven in mind as we approach his music for the first time: the tireless and patient craftsman. The truth is, Beethoven worked tremendously hard at his art. For perhaps fifty of his fifty-six years, he arose daily to begin the laborious task of carving his music out of the noise and chaos that surrounded him. As a child he was a virtual slave to his keyboard; as a young man, a tireless student of counterpoint, orchestration, piano technique. And no other composer left such a complete record of sketches and ideas considered, abandoned, taken up again, worked out, then transformed into sonatas, symphonies, string quartets. Beethoven did not sit under a tree, writing down inspired music as fast as it came to him. Imagine instead a prematurely middle-aged man, often sick, crouched over a messy desk at midnight, spectacles on, tossing one scrap of paper after another onto the floor in the search for just the right note and the perfect texture.

His exacting work methods ensured that Beethoven would not be an especially prolific composer. Compared with Haydn's 104 and Mozart's forty-one symphonies, Beethoven's numbered a mere nine. Five piano concertos, one opera, thirty-two piano sonatas, sixteen string quartets, and an assortment of other chamber and orchestral works make up the rest of the Beethoven canon. However, each piece in the list impacts in a way few others could. The Ninth Symphony is about four times the length of any one of Karl Dittersdorf's symphonic efforts but has the emotional power of all of them put together.

It is not just in his dedication to hard work that Beethoven was very much a man of this world. For the most part, he lived a life bounded by the same restrictions and realities as those of most of his contemporaries. If he is portrayed as a Byronic hero, a poetic figure of romance and artistic integrity, he was also a man who suffered from chronic diarrhea, struggled to pay his rent on time, stared after attractive women in the street and was fond of his wine. It is a tribute to Beethoven's genius, not a repudiation of it, to look squarely in the face of the man with all his faults, difficulties and tragedies. Beethoven's story is no less compelling when it is understood to be the tale of a man, rather than that of a demigod.

In just the same way, Beethoven's music is more approachable than you might think and responds extremely well to analysis. As well as being a powerful document of an age and the testament of a great mind, it is also constructed according to rules and techniques you can hear for yourself with relative ease. As understanding Beethoven's humanity does not rob you of the Beethoven myth, so understanding the music takes away none of its power and beauty. The more you appreciate how Beethoven achieved his magical control over his material, the more remarkable his talent becomes.

The great Beethoven can belong to you with just a little help and a few simple guidelines. He may seem an impossibly inaccessible mountain from a distance, forbidding and challenging, but at the foot of the peak, there is a path to the summit. Let's take the first step.

2

Listening with Your Heart, Listening with Your Mind

A t its center, classical music is just like every other kind of music. It aims to charm us with the beauty of its melodies, move us with the force of its rhythms and seduce us with the suggestive power of its texture. Music is the most natural of all the arts, and its appreciation takes place deep within our subconscious. We respond to all music, classical included, instinctively. The right combination of sounds can move us to tears, exalt us to spiritual heights or urge our bodies to move in mysterious harmony to its beat. Music's power over us derives from this semi-mystical, unwilled source.

Beethoven's is among the most elemental music ever composed. As we shall see in more detail as we investigate his music, one of the secrets of his art was his use of the most basic musical elements in the construction of his works. Even those who have heard only a few notes of Beethoven's music — the opening *da-da-da-duh* of the Fifth Symphony — already have a clue to his obsessive use of simple rhythmic patterns. His melodies share the same elemental nature. On the most basic level of musical appreciation, Beethoven needs no introduction. His music easily speaks for itself.

But classical music has more than one level of meaning. That is one of its joys. You can listen to a piece of classical music over and over again and never hear the same thing twice. It is a complex and intricate art that appeals to our intellect as well as to our emotions. It is a kind of music in which form — the organization of the piece itself — plays a significant part in its overall impact. If you want to really understand classical music, you have to know a bit about form.

Music is a formal as well as an expressive art. The design of a piece of music is not just a package for the expressive message inside; the design itself has an expressive quality, too. The composer often puts as much of his or her soul and heart into the form as into the content — form and content merge in this respect. And, as we will see, this is especially true of Beethoven. There is no way you can fully connect with his music without being sensitive to its design.

All music — from the most complex symphony to the simplest folk song — has form, in the same way that every bit of prose has some organization, whether it's a memo, a letter or a novel. However, hearing the form is not always a natural response to the music. The form of a piece, although not hidden away, may not be immediately apprehended. The problem for new classical listeners is that most of the music they're used to — pop music — has a very rudimentary form that won't help them tackle the more complex structures of the classics. As well, pop music aims to make an immediate impact on its listeners. We can get addicted to pop's jolt-per-minute ratio and lose the ability to cover a larger and more complex musical terrain.

So the first step in listening to Beethoven, or any other classical composer, is to treat the music not as a rock video but as a feature film. Give it time to make its point and unravel its mysteries. Not everything is on the surface of a good film, nor is it in classical music. Classical composers expected their audiences to follow the "plot" of their works and built surprises and suspense into them for that reason. You must give the music a chance to show what it can do.

And don't be discouraged if at first your attention begins to wander. Just wait for the music to engage you again. Like anything else, your concentration and enjoyment will improve with practice. The more you listen to the music, the more you will be able to hear within it. Classical music is mysterious in this regard. Your enjoyment of the classics, unlike your appreciation of pop music, increases with each repetition. There's always something new to hear, both on the surface and in the beauties of the design.

A basic psychological fact lies at the heart of all considerations of musical form: aural memory is short. It may be an inborn trait or a result of living in a fundamentally visual age, but people have a hard time remembering sounds. Most of us can remember a face (something visual) much longer than its accompanying name (something aural). Consequently, the only way to create a comprehensible musical design over time — a form — is through repetition. It may seem obvious, but it's worth noting that repetition is the key to musical organization.

Just as there are lots of ways to repeat a verbal idea, there are lots of ways to repeat a musical idea, and the history of musical form is the history of the different techniques that composers have invented to do just that. So before we see how Beethoven created the formal side of his music, let's look at a very simple folk song to understand why form is so important in music.

Do you remember the little folk song *Au clair de la lune?* It begins "Au clair de la lune, mon ami Pierrot. . . ." Or in English:

In the silver moonlight, my good friend Pierrot,
Pen and paper lend me, do not say me "No."
Burnt out is my candle, cold my fire and grey;
By our Lady's mercy, take me in, I pray.

If you're not familiar with the title or lyrics, you probably know the melody: *do-do-do-re-mi — re — do-mi-re-re-do.*

Hum the tune to yourself or play it on a piano and see if you can spot its organization. It's actually quite simple and is typical of thousands of folk songs as well as many art pieces. A line is played twice, then followed by a different bit of music and then played again. Musicologists have labeled this pattern *aaba*. Listen to or hum *Au clair de la lune* again to make sure you can hear that *aaba* pattern. The first two and the last lines are made up of exactly the same notes; only the third line is different.

This simple tune is worth a little of our time, because it contains principles of musical organization and clues for listening that extend far beyond its brief forty-four-note compass.

Hum the first line to yourself again. That line represents a musical sentence, or idea — a tiny musical organization that has a certain integrity and shape that will allow you to recognize it every time it appears in a piece. In this respect, it is identical to the opening of a Beethoven symphony or a Mozart string quartet, or any other piece of classical music. All music is made up of these musical sentences or ideas. Learning to recognize them is half the battle in listening to classical music.

Creating memorable musical ideas is the composer's first and most basic task, and it isn't as simple as it may seem. Since musical memory is short, it is easy to forget a series of notes once it has disappeared. Somehow the phrase must be made to stick in the listener's mind.

Every memorable musical idea has an identifiable rhythm, a simple organization of beats that you can tap with your finger and recall easily. Listen to any kind of music. The melodies you remember and sing afterward all have a clear rhythmic organization. Try it with *Au clair de la lune*. Tap out the rhythm of that first line. It's very simple, very straightforward, easily remembered and identified. Since rhythm is the most basic musical element, the one we hear most viscerally, every musical idea must have a rhythmic shape.

All classical composers were alert to the rhythmic organization of their compositions, but none more so than Beethoven. Rhythm is such an important element in Beethoven's music that it sometimes dwarfs all the other elements. Think of the opening of the *Moonlight* Sonata or the famous *da-da-da-dum* of the Fifth Symphony. In these instances, the musical idea at the heart of the piece is almost exclusively a rhythm. The actual notes set to the rhythm are less important.

Rhythm is not the only tool with which composers create memorable musical ideas. Melodic shape — the patterns of ups and downs in a melody — also became an extremely important technique for composers in the classical tradition. They discovered that small changes in the shape of melodies had immense musical and psychological impact on audiences. Whole books, in fact, have been written on the psychological "meaning" of different melodic patterns. Even in a tune as simple as *Au clair de la lune*, we can see these musical and psychological forces at work.

Compare the two musical phrases that make up the folk song. The first phrase, the one repeated in lines 1, 2 and 4, revolves around a narrow orbit of three notes, ascending and descending its melodic staircase a couple of times. The narrow compass of the melody creates a psychological feeling of security and safety. In contrast, the second musical idea (line 3) covers a wider field of action (five notes) and includes two big leaps (from *my* to *candle* and back down again to *cold*). It also descends to the lowest note of the piece — on the word *gray* — and the ear is always sensitive to the highest and lowest notes in a melody. A more free-ranging line like this one creates a sense of adventure and daring in music simply by the arrangement of its notes. This simple third line provides exactly the kind of contrast that makes for balance and unity in a piece, and allows us to hear this famous tune again and again with satisfaction and enjoyment.

Most of the musical effects of *Au clair de la lune* are subliminal, operating just below the level of consciousness. Much classical music operates in the same way. Yet analyzing these effects helps us become more sensitive to them. When you become more familiar with classical music, you will hear the shape and rhythm of its phrases naturally and spontaneously. For now, however, take the time to listen for the rhythmic and melodic character of music that you know well. Take your favorite pieces of pop or classical music and try to detect the structure of their musical ideas. It's a painless way of training yourself to hear the basic phrases from which all music is constructed. Those little musical packages are the sentences from which great composers build paragraphs, chapters and finally complete musical stories. You need to be able to recognize them in order to follow the storylines.

Always ready to make things a little easier for you, composers have adopted a convention to help you pick out the first and generally the most important musical idea in any piece. Ninety-nine times out of a hundred, the key musical idea in a work will be the first set of notes you hear. In music, there is no time for the trick openings and false clues that filmmakers and novelists adore. Occasionally, a classical work or even one of its movements has a slow introduction, obviously set apart from the rest by its tempo, but generally the piece just jumps right into the action with its first, central musical idea. Practice listening to classical music this way: focus your attention on the first musical idea you hear — it may be only a few seconds long — and then listen to see whether that idea is repeated or a new one introduced. You'll be able to spot the new idea because its rhythm and melody will be different. Perhaps a third idea or a fourth will be presented before that first idea is repeated. See if you can pick out that first idea every time it recurs: follow that musical trail, don't let it out of earshot. It is out of those little ideas and their succession that musical form is crafted. Once you get used to hearing the ideas, you can learn to be sensitive to their order and placement. That's when things start to get interesting.

Let's return to *Au clair de la lune* for our first lesson in the beauties of form. Hearing the musical ideas in this folk song is easy. As mentioned, there are only two: one repeated in lines 1, 2 and 4, and a second appearing only in line 3. Each of these two ideas has its own musical interest, and on one level we can appreciate the song for these individual ideas alone. Form, however, allows us a second order of beauty, one that derives from the perfect organization of individual segments and parts.

Compare the first and last lines of *Au clair de la lune*. On one level they are identical, made up of the same notes, played in the same rhythm, causing the same pattern of sound waves to reach our ears and be processed by our brains. One might assume, therefore, that the two lines of music will create an identical emotional impression.

But they don't. Some people hear the last line as a sadder version of the first, a wistful reminiscence of the musical idea. Others feel it is more defiant, a bold restatement of the original premise. Few listeners feel it has exactly the same emotional coloration it had at the beginning of the tune. The interposition of the second, more open, idea has forced us to hear the first in a new way. Form has entered into our musical universe. Not just the ideas, but their order has emotional and musical significance.

In this respect, music is much like film, especially the cinematic technique called montage. The great Russian director Sergei

Eisenstein, a man very sensitive to music in his films, was the inventor of montage. Eisenstein realized the power of succession in film images after trying an experiment. He interposed a neutral shot of a man's face among a sequence of other shots: of a baby crying, people arguing, and a woman standing in a landscape. Although the man's face was identical in every shot, Eisenstein's audiences interpreted it in wildly different ways. They thought the man looked angry after the argument, anxious after the crying baby and transfixed by love after the appearance of the woman. What Eisenstein discovered in film, composers had unconsciously known for centuries. Emotional power does not consist just in a striking individual image or idea. It is the combination of images that makes for real beauty — their organization, their form.

To cement that idea let's return one last time to *Au Clair de la lune* and experiment with the dynamics — the louds and softs — in the piece. Dynamic contrasts immediately create correspondences with the human speaking voice, the source of so much musical significance. Loud music is interpreted like loud speech, to represent pride, anger or determination. Soft music is the domain of shyness, tenderness and intimacy. Changes in dynamic level are a key to the changing emotional temperature within a piece of music.

Try it with *Au clair de la lune*. Sing the whole thing very softly, then very loudly. Then change the dynamics line by line, with a loud first line and a soft last one. Or the reverse. You'll notice that each variation in dynamics has given the piece a slightly different emotional character, because with each you have subtly changed its form, the meaning of its organization. Is the second line a less confident echo of the first or an affirmation of it, gaining in authority with repetition? How should the new idea in the third line be expressed, with confidence or foreboding? And the return of the first line — always a major musical and emotional event — how is it to be understood?

All these are questions of form, and while they may be a bit silly when confined to a simple four-line folk song, they lie at the heart of our understanding of great classical music. The meaning of Beethoven's music — which has been a matter of intense debate for more than two centuries — depends on differing interpretations of the emotions inspired by both its ideas and its organization. To appreciate all that classical music has to offer, you need to become familiar with the succession of musical ideas and their relationship to one another. Then the second level of beauty in music will open up to you like a blossom.

Au clair de la lune has given us just a taste of the role of form in music. Let's bring on Beethoven now and start our listening to the real thing.

3

Operating Manual: *Für Elise*

I n late April of 1810, a beautiful Viennese noblewoman, Therese Malfatti, opened a letter addressed to her and watched as a piece of music fluttered out of the envelope and onto the floor. She leaned to pick it up and saw that it was labeled simply: "For Therese."

The scrawled handwriting on the manuscript was immediately familiar to her; it belonged to her suitor, Ludwig van Beethoven. A few months shy of his fortieth birthday and increasingly desperate to marry, Beethoven had fallen in love with Therese earlier that spring and had proposed. The marriage never took place for reasons unclear, although it seems that Therese was willing, but her family was not.

This little story is worth repeating, because when the music was found many years later among Therese's effects, its dedication was mistakenly read as "Für Elise," and the piece has been known by that title to this day. This, perhaps one of Beethoven's best-known pieces, was thus no trifle for its composer but a musical love note or, more likely, a musical farewell to a doomed love affair.

It is also a perfect introduction to Beethoven's musical language.

Don't be nervous as you approach a piece of classical music. You have all the tools you need to appreciate it. If you could work your way through *Au clair de la lune*, you'll find nothing daunting in *Für*

Elise. With practice, you'll be able to pick out all the details that make classical music so enjoyable. These music chapters are intended as nothing more than a guided tour of some of the more significant landmarks in the pieces they investigate. Eventually, you'll need no guide.

Here's how I suggest you use the chapters that focus on musical analysis. Start by obtaining a recording of the works — there are probably dozens to choose from. A CD is the easiest format to work with. Read the chapter with the CD in the player, preferably with your hand near the "pause" button so you can start and stop the music at will. Don't be afraid to stop when you lose interest in the music, or when you're not sure where you are. Nor should you hesitate to forget about reading the chapter and just listen to the music. There's no right or wrong way to listen to classical music. Eventually, you'll get out of the music what you want. The music is patient; it will wait for you a lifetime.

With that in mind, let's look at the musical form, or "plot," of *Für Elise*. Its structure is fairly simple. Musicologists call it a sectional form. All that means is that a main idea is repeated several times with different musical sections interspersed between the repeats. It is a basic musical form, in fact an expanded version of the organization of *Au clair de la lune*. But, as we have seen with that folk song, the simple notion of return always has significant emotional consequences in music.

You will want to pay particular attention to the first bit of music you hear in *Für Elise*. As with any classical piece, the most important music here — the phrase that identifies the piece almost instantly, sets its emotional tone and provides a formal framework — occurs right at the beginning.

Listen to this opening phrase (you probably already know it). It begins with an easy-to-distinguish alternation of two notes half a tone apart: a slow trill. Whenever you hear that two-note pattern, your ear should sense a return to the main idea the way you sense an impending storm by a slight change in the wind. This little musical molecule is the building block from which the entire cellular structure of *Für Elise* is created. Like a strand of DNA, this theme winds itself around and through the piece, imparting to it its character, form and meaning.

It is always a chancy proposition to try to describe music and its effects on listeners, as music is a form of communication that usually transcends words. Nonetheless, I think it's safe to note the flowing quality of this main theme of *Für Elise*. A tiny cascade of notes like drops of water is followed and balanced by two gentle upward waves of music; then the cycle repeats.

This musical idea seems to have had an almost obsessive fascination for Beethoven. The main theme — the first idea — is made up of two repetitions of the trill figure and two repetitions of the arpeggio, the upwardly flowing figure. This whole package is then repeated. Then Beethoven repeats the rhythm of the second half of the idea as a brief respite before returning to the two-note opening again through a series of repeated notes in various octaves, which turns into the opening trill almost without even realizing it. This entire second section is played again. In all, within the first sixty seconds of *Für Elise*, Beethoven replays that opening trill idea eight times.

At last, Beethoven changes gears and introduces a new musical thought — listen for the melody that is introduced by three chords in the right hand. It's important for your appreciation of *Für Elise* to recognize the beginning of this second section and understand it as a turn away from the mood and music of the opening. Beethoven has done a lot to help you identify this change in musical direction. The second theme is in a new key and has a major, happy sound as opposed to the brooding minor of the opening. The flowing quality of the opening has changed to a different texture: a rolling figure in the left hand accompanies a new melody in the right, almost like a band providing backup to a lead singer. Where the first theme was somewhat claustrophobic, constantly returning to itself, this second theme is more open and generous.

The melody at the beginning of this section, once established, gives way to a quick succession of notes in the right hand, repeated twice, which then abruptly slows down, like a runaway team reined in by a frantic driver. In an instant, the mood changes and this section is transformed back into the bleak terrain outlined by the main theme.

This stark transition has a powerful effect, even in a piece this small. The happier mood of the second section, to which we were just beginning to respond, disappears, and the pensive, repetitive character of the opening returns, like a thought Beethoven can't shake, no matter how hard he tries.

We noted in the last chapter that in the hands of classical composers, repetition was never a mechanical business of replaying identical notes and harmonies just for the sake of form. Repetition in a classical piece signals the return of an earlier idea. It is almost always used as a psychological and dramatic device, as it is here in *Für Elise*. The abruptness with which the second idea evaporates back into the first imparts an emotional meaning to the music that is quite telling. Few composers understood the art of musical drama as did Beethoven. The mere act of placing two musical ideas in a certain relationship creates a connection between the composer and the listener.

On its return, the first idea is replayed almost exactly as we first heard it, though without the repeats, and then another new idea appears. This time, however, Beethoven does not provide a contrast to the mood of his first idea but an intensification of it. This third idea flows so smoothly from the main theme that for a moment you may not realize you're into a new section. This is exactly what Beethoven wants — to erase the seam between musical ideas that often slows a piece down, and to heighten rather than undermine the prevailing mood.

The key to the beginning of the third section is the repeated note that starts hammering away in the bass like a muffled drum beat. It is the final note of the main theme that preceded it, now drawn out to provide the foundation for the next section.

That repeated note provides the intensification of mood that Beethoven wants for this section. A repeated note in music is like nailing a melody to the floor. No matter how much the music may wish to develop and travel, the constantly repeating note won't let it budge, always bringing it back to a single, unyielding point. It is the tensest device in music. The melody in the right hand, which begins with a dramatic diminished chord, is not bad, but it doesn't get a chance to develop. Our attention is always drawn to the bass and that tolling single note.

Beethoven begins to repeat this section with the same chords in the right hand and that same note drumming ominously in the bass, when he suddenly introduces a favorite trick — a Beethoven trademark. Rather than continue exactly as before, the bass note moves up a step, the minor harmony abruptly turns major, and the idea briefly goes off in a quite different direction before coming to a suspenseful, inconclusive finish. That quick change when the audience least expects it is a device Beethoven used throughout his composing career. He loved the element of surprise and resulting shock such moments provided. A whole treatise could be written — probably has been written — on the element of surprise in the music of Beethoven. You'll notice it again and again as you become more familiar with his work. It is one of the bases of his reputation as a dramatic composer.

Beethoven keeps us in suspense for a bar or two at the end of this section as we await the next musical idea. He buys time with a single arpeggiated (broken) chord that ranges over the entire keyboard in a strangely somnambulistic mood, before a descending scale leads us back to the first theme. That theme, without repeats, is heard one last time, and *Für Elise* comes to a hushed, moving close.

For such a simple work, *Für Elise* packs quite a punch. Beethoven may have been sparing in texture and simple in musical plot, but this delicate miniature leaves a clear emotional impression. One of the fascinations of classical music is its ability to create this kind of impression, meaning that goes beyond the sheer physical enjoyment of the sounds. If you doubt this, imagine what Therese Malfatti must have felt, seated at the forte-piano, as she played this piece over for the first time. But even if you had never heard of Therese and knew nothing of the circumstances surrounding the composition of this work, it would still have meaning for you — a purely musical, rather than biographical, significance.

As mentioned, the key to appreciating this meaning is in hearing the design of the music and recognizing the clues composers leave to explain it. We will be noting these clues throughout this book, because practice in spotting them will allow you to follow a musical story. Beethoven wrote his music with the expectation that his audiences would be sensitive to his musical structure. So in *Für Elise*, as in the rest of his music, train yourself to listen for changes in mood, melody or key. What might at first have seemed an undifferentiated mass of notes will begin to take on shape and form. There is a thrill in being able to hear the musical pattern for yourself. Music you might have been familiar with on one level bursts onto another right before your ears.

Beethoven's music seems to reach out through the notes to leave a personal message with his audiences. This is true of his most powerful works as well as of miniatures like *Für Elise*. It is thus impossible to listen to Beethoven's music without becoming curious about the man who wrote it. And the full story of that man is as fascinating and complex as the music itself. Beethoven was not a simple character, and his life was not a simple life. Bound up in his passions, difficulties and misfortunes are the raw materials from which the music was made.

4

The Young Beethoven

Beethoven was born into a Europe on the brink of political revolution, into a country just emerging as a cultural force and into a tortured and troubled family. These three influences — political, cultural and familial — were to play heavily in Beethoven's life. Each contributed to his personality and, ultimately, to his music.

He came into the world on December 16, 1770, born to Johann and Maria van Beethoven in the back part of a rented house in Bonn. Then as now, Bonn was a delightful town situated on the Rhine River, set in beautiful natural surroundings, a center of cultural excellence. In the late eighteenth century, Germany was organized into innumerable small towns, each controlled by a secular or ecclesiastical prince. Bonn had been an ecclesiastical principality — the seat of the Elector of Cologne — since the thirteenth century and had developed an extensive musical and theatrical life. The Elector at Beethoven's birth, Max Freidrich, may have been a man of the church, but he was also a generous patron of the arts.

The Elector's musical establishment was the professional home of both Beethoven's father and grandfather, as it would be briefly for Beethoven himself. Johann was a tenor in the Elector's musical entourage, only a middling tenor by all accounts, but Beethoven's grandfather was the Elector's *Kapellmeister* (chapel master), the chief musician in Bonn. With an orchestra, two choirs and a private opera company to supervise and lead, the *Kapellmeister* was an extremely significant person in the ecclesiastical capital. It was grandfather Ludwig, after whom Beethoven was named, who was the reason the Beethovens were in Germany at all. Without him, Ludwig van Beethoven might have been the crowning glory of Belgian, not German, music.

The Beethoven family had lived near the village of Malines, in Flanders, at least as far back as the Renaissance. Business was their occupation: they had traded in lace, fine furniture and wine. Grandfather Ludwig was the first musician in the family, and when the Elector of Liège, the local prince, became the Elector of Cologne in 1733, he asked Ludwig to come with him to his new capital, Bonn, to sing in his church choir. So the Beethovens became established in Germany.

Beethoven retained fond impressions of his grandfather, even though he died when the composer was only three. He carried his grandfather's portrait with him throughout his life. Every time he changed residences in Vienna (more than twenty-five times in all), the portrait went along and was one of the first things unpacked. The talismanic significance of this picture was critical to Beethoven. It represented probity, honesty, success — everything his grandfather had stood for and his father had not.

Beethoven's relationship to his father was the central formative influence in his early years. The shadow of those years fell heavily on the rest of Beethoven's life; the wounds his father inflicted never entirely healed. Johann van Beethoven had started life with some promise. The son of one of Bonn's most successful musicians, he became a musician himself. At first he did well, both as a singer and as a teacher of some of Bonn's most illustrious young people. But something happened to Johann, and he started to drink. By the time of his marriage, in 1767, his fondness for the bottle was well known, although how serious his addiction was at that time is not clear. His bride, Maria Magdalena Keverich, Beethoven's mother, may have had a year or so of happiness at the beginning of her marriage, but that vanished when her first child died soon after his birth in 1769. Maybe that sad event also pushed Johann over the edge, for it is after this period that stories proliferate of his drunkenness and abuse. He spent more and more time at the tavern, staying away from home all day and often all night. His drinking debts mounted, plunging his family into a desperate poverty from which they would never escape. He began to be known as the town drunk. Maria attempted to remonstrate with him but to no avail. It fell to her to manage the meager resources that Johann's dwindling income left them.

We know very little about Beethoven's mother; only one or two of her comments survive. "If you want to take my good advice," she apparently said one day to Cäcilia Fischer, her landlady's daughter, "remain single, and then you will have the most tranquil, most beautiful, most pleasurable life. For what is marriage? A little joy, but then a chain of sorrows." Cäcilia confided many years later that she had never seen Frau Beethoven laugh.

The deterioration of the Beethoven household seems to have been far advanced by the time Ludwig was born, despite hopes that his birth might prove an antidote to Johann's increasing despair. Johann van Beethoven exercised a virtual reign of terror over his imprisoned family. Violence, or the threat of violence, was a constant presence. Worse was the unpredictability of its outbreak and the anxious waiting for the inevitable rage to flare again. In such households love blossoms in poignant ways: moments of affection stolen between bouts of anger; guilt flooding after rage as love fights with hate. In the words of Maria Magdalena van Beethoven, "a little joy, but then a chain of sorrows."

Admittedly, our knowledge of this period of Beethoven's life is extremely sketchy, based on observations and recollections of neighbors made many years after the fact. Beethoven never spoke about his childhood. Indeed, even Johann's alcoholism, especially at this period, is contested by some biographers. But although the details are missing, the broad outline of Beethoven's early years is clear enough. It was, for him, a time of pain.

Beethoven's musical talent, not surprisingly, began to show itself by the time he was three or four, and Johann was quick to try to develop and exploit it. But Johann was no Leopold Mozart, well-known musician and pedagogue. He may have had some teaching ability, but his overriding concern was to market his son's musical talent as early as possible. His teaching methods — if they can be called that — seem to have been based on forcing Ludwig to the keyboard as often and for as long as possible. Johann would constantly resort to violence in imposing his will on his son. "There were few days when he was not beaten in order to compel him to set himself at the piano," wrote one family friend. Cäcilia Fischer remembered Beethoven many years later as "a little boy, standing on a little footstool in front of the clavier to which the implacable severity of his father had so early condemned him, weeping."

The regimen to which Beethoven was submitted was unyielding. Music and practicing were virtually his whole life from the time he was four or five. He had only a few years of formal schooling, leaving elementary school when he was eleven. Such an upbringing was bound to scar a young child whose soul was as sensitive and open as Beethoven's. He reacted as one might expect, by withdrawing into a cold and embarrassed silence. His schoolmates noticed nothing remarkable about Beethoven except his slovenly appearance, which seems to have characterized him from the time he was about nine. In later years, they would comment with amazement on how little indication the young Beethoven gave of the world-famous figure he was to become. One teacher noted that he was "a shy and taciturn boy, observing more and pondering more than he spoke." Another contemporary noted that "outside of music, he understood nothing of social life; consequently he was ill-humored with other people, did not know how to converse with them, and withdrew into himself, so that he was looked upon as a misanthrope." These descriptions of Beethoven as a schoolboy eerily echo almost identical remarks made decades later about the grown man.

His solace, even at this early age, was solitude and the comfort of nature. "His happiest hours were those when he was free of all company," wrote Gottfried Fischer, Cäcilia's brother, "when his parents were all away and he was left alone by himself." During those times, Beethoven would spend hours at the window, enjoying especially the view of the Rhine from the back of the house. Cäcilia Fischer came across the young Beethoven one day "leaning in the window with his head in his hands and staring fixedly at one spot. He said, 'I was just occupied with such a lovely, deep thought, I couldn't bear to be disturbed.'" Whether it created or merely intensified a natural independence, his father's erratic behavior accelerated Beethoven's desire to escape to a better world, one he might create through his art.

By the time Beethoven was nine, his father had realized his own limitations as a teacher and found instruction for the boy among the more reputable musicians of Bonn. Chief among these was Christian Gottlob Neefe, a quite accomplished musician who had journeyed to Bonn in 1781 to supervise the music in Elector Max Freidrich's newly created theater company, as well as play the organ in the electoral chapel. Neefe may have been the first person with whom Beethoven came into contact who revealed to him the possibility of a life that was not banal, sordid and unhappy. Neefe was also something of an intellectual and talked with Beethoven about the new ideas sweeping the world as well as instructing him in music. Although limited somewhat as a teacher, Neefe gave Beethoven the bulk of his musical instruction for a decade.

He also helped Beethoven's career in a way Johann seemed incapable of doing. Johann had attempted to display his precocious son, à la Mozart, once when Beethoven was eight but never tried to do so again. Neefe, on the other hand, occasionally allowed Beethoven to take over his organist's duties when he was only twelve, and two years later, in 1784, sponsored him to a paid position in the Elector's musical entourage. It was the beginning of a varied career for Beethoven in the electoral court, which would include playing the viola in the court opera pit, teaching a few pupils and acting as piano soloist with the electoral orchestra.

Neefe provided Beethoven with more than just intellectual and musical stimulation. Through Neefe, Beethoven became acquainted with a number of sophisticated and wealthy noble families who provided the artistic nourishment for Bonn's many musicians and actors. One family in particular, the von Breunings, proved critical to Beethoven's intellectual and personal development.

The von Breunings were an established noble family of court councillors and educators who had lived in Bonn for over thirty years when Beethoven met them in 1782, probably introduced by Neefe. Emmanuel von Breuning had died five years earlier. His widow, Helene von Breuning, was perhaps the most important woman in Beethoven's young life next to his own mother. Helene had four children, two of whom became Beethoven's lifelong friends: Eleonore, a year older than Beethoven, and Stephan, two years younger. Beethoven entered the house as piano teacher to the two youngest children and stayed on as a surrogate member of the family.

What a remarkable contrast to his own home the impressionable young musician found in the magnificent von Breuning mansion. Instead of debts, recriminations and the cramped psychology of fear, here was light and charm and talk of philosophy, art and politics. As Franz Wegeler, a young man in the von Breuning entourage, who became Beethoven's most enduring friend, put it:

Ludwig received his first acquaintance with German literature, especially poetry, as well as his first training in social behavior in the midst of the von Breuning family. In this house reigned an unconstrained tone of culture in spite of youthful willfulness. . . . When we add that the family possessed considerable wealth, especially before the war, it will be easy to understand that the first joyous emotions of Beethoven found vent here. Soon he was treated as one of the children in the family, spending in the house not only the greater part of his days, but also many nights. Here he felt he was free, here he moved about without constraint, everything conspired to make him cheerful and develop his mind.

It was not just hospitality and culture that Beethoven found in the circle of light the von Breunings offered. Here Beethoven's talent brought him into contact with the musical elite of Bonn, especially Count Ferdinand Waldstein, who had arrived in Bonn in 1788. Waldstein was an intimate friend of Max Franz, the Elector, and was well connected in the imperial capital, Vienna. Waldstein took an immediate interest in the young Beethoven, now just beginning to try his hand at composition, and became a lifelong champion of his work. He also provided a focus for Beethoven's growing interest in the intellectual and political ideas of the Enlightenment, the period that produced Kant's philosophy, Goethe's and Schiller's literature, and the French Revolution.

The Enlightenment — a very large term encompassing a wide variety of ideas and impulses — was Western Europe's excited embrace of the growing power and strength of science and rationality. Gathering confidence from the scientific discoveries of Galileo and others in the late Renaissance, Enlightenment thinkers encouraged humanity to shake off the superstitions of the past and use its own reason to create an earthly life subject to no master but itself. This humanity-centered philosophy had powerful repercussions throughout Europe. Politically, it led to the French Revolution, as it held up reason and natural, spontaneous feeling as the basis of political power, not position and prestige. Socially and culturally, its effects may have been even more profound. Enlightenment philosophers taught that true human nobility came from inner resources, not outer; that real worth was based on a person's character and his or her efforts to reach the highest goals.

Under Max Franz, Bonn became a center for Enlightenment thought. A university was created, devoted to the latest advances in all branches of learning. Reading societies abounded, in which the latest ideas were discussed and passionately debated. Many of Beethoven's closest friends and associates were involved with these societies. Inevitably, the young Beethoven, now in his teens, was also drawn to the nobility and excitement of Enlightenment ideals.

Beethoven was never an especially original social and political thinker, although he was a passionate defender of the ideas he borrowed and learned from others. But he did not embrace Enlightenment ideas just for convention's sake; they reverberated deeply within his own soul. This philosophy must have seemed thrilling to the young composer. It would have been exactly what Beethoven, given his own personal situation, needed to hear.

Many of the young men and women of Europe who were attracted to the Enlightenment were children of privilege whose dedication to the philosophy was primarily intellectual. Not so Beethoven. He knew first-hand how circumstance and fate could conspire to limit an individual's potential. Early on, Beethoven developed a longing for a better kind of life than the one he led, a life of virtue, art and beauty. His desire for this life, his hope of attaining it and his attempts to enter it became an essential part of his biography. Unlike his more affluent contemporaries, Beethoven lived the ideals of the Enlightenment, which is perhaps why he never wavered in his dedication to this philosophy of liberation, and why his music speaks so powerfully of achievement, struggle and joy.

Under the tutelage of Neefe and within the welcoming embrace of the von Breuning household, Beethoven's musical genius began to explode. With each passing year, his skill on the pianoforte and his budding attempts at composition won him greater and greater praise. Finally, when he was seventeen, it became clear that the musical community of Bonn had become too confining for the powerful young performer. In 1787, he was sent to Vienna to study with the greatest musician of the day, Wolfgang Amadeus Mozart.

The pairing of the mature Mozart and the young Beethoven was all too brief. Beethoven probably had only a lesson or two from Mozart, but it was enough to earn him Mozart's now-famous recommendation. "Keep your eyes on him," he told a friend, "some day he will give the world something to talk about." Beethoven was anxious to continue his studies in the imperial capital, but a longer stay in Vienna proved impossible. After just a few weeks, Beethoven was summoned home. His mother had fallen gravely ill; within two months she was dead.

Beethoven's relationship to his mother has been the subject of much speculation over the years. Some commentators assume that Beethoven rejected her, and consequently all women, because of her failure to protect him from the violence and abuse of his father. More likely, Beethoven and his mother, equally victimized, formed something of a conspiratorial alliance. Although the adult Beethoven as a rule avoided conversation about his youth, throughout his life he spoke lovingly of his mother. His friends of later years agree that he remembered her "with love and feeling, calling her often an honest, good-hearted woman" (Franz Wegeler). Beethoven was probably speaking the truth when he said, "She was such a kind, loving mother to me, and my best friend."

The death of wife and mother had predictable ramifications in the

Beethoven family. Johann sank even deeper into an alcoholic haze, his condition deteriorating so rapidly that Beethoven was forced to petition the Elector to remove his father from further service. Johann's salary was given to Beethoven so he could look after his two younger brothers. At nineteen, Beethoven had become the official head of his household. Johann spent the remainder of his days in a pathetic state. Stephan von Breuning remembered later seeing Beethoven one night pleading with a police officer determined to arrest Johann for drunkenness. Virtually every night, either Beethoven or one of his brothers would have to collect their father from the local tavern.

In an odd way, this double loss — of his mother to death and his father to alcoholism — liberated Beethoven. He was now a young man, no longer a youth, with almost a decade of professional music making behind him and rosier prospects ahead. He started composing in earnest, and though few of these works are performed today, he wrote about fifty pieces in the next three years. As a pianist, Beethoven's reputation was beginning to spread beyond the borders of his home town. The Elector's orchestra, with Beethoven as soloist, had undertaken a concert tour up and down the Rhine in the summer of 1790, and Beethoven had amazed audiences with his skill on the piano. A columnist for a musical journal, reporting on the trip, noted:

> I heard also one of the greatest of pianists — the dear, good Beethoven. . . . The greatness of this amiable, light-hearted man, as a virtuoso, may be safely estimated from his almost inexhaustible wealth of ideas, the altogether characteristic style of expression in his playing, and the great execution which he displays. I know, therefore, of no one thing that he lacks, that conduces to the greatness of an artist.

Beethoven's growing maturity was being nurtured on the home

front by Helene von Breuning. After the death of Beethoven's mother, the von Breuning household became a first rather than a second home for the young man. Helene had already noticed a wild streak in Beethoven's personality and sought to tame it. When Beethoven would try to find any possible excuse to cancel a lesson (he hated teaching), Helene would insist he honor his commitments. She taught him to distinguish solid criticism from fawning flattery and helped instil the confidence she knew he would need when he left Bonn.

As Beethoven entered his twenty-second year, in 1792, it became clear to his friends and admirers that there was nothing left for him in Bonn. To continue his education, he would need another sojourn in Vienna. Mozart had, unfortunately, died the year before, but Austria's most famous living musician, Joseph Haydn, was willing to accept Beethoven as a pupil. Haydn had met Beethoven earlier that year on a trip through Bonn and had been impressed by several of Beethoven's compositions. Urged on by Waldstein and Neefe, the Elector agreed to pay for Beethoven to go to Vienna for a short period to study with Haydn.

In the autograph album Beethoven received as a parting gift, Count Waldstein penned one of the most prophetic comments in the history of Western music:

> Dear Beethoven! You are going to Vienna in fulfillment of your
> long frustrated wishes. The Genius of Mozart is mourning and
> weeping over the death of her pupil. She found a refuge but no
> occupation with the inexhaustible Haydn; through him she
> wishes to form a union with another. With the help of assiduous
> labor you shall receive Mozart's spirit from Haydn's hands.

Beethoven left Bonn in November of 1792. He took with him his own genius and as much musical experience and education as the Rhenish capital could provide. He also carried with him a personal philosophy, an Enlightenment fire that never stopped burning, even when it was extinguished throughout the rest of Europe. His final baggage was perhaps the heaviest: the memories of his troubled family. The strains and fissures of his upbringing — faults in his personal geology — were to cause many an emotional cave-in in the years to follow. Yet Beethoven approached his future with confidence, although little did he suspect as he left Bonn that he would never return. He was in fact heading toward the city that would be his home for the rest of his life — Vienna.

5

"Mozart's Spirit from Haydn's Hands"

When Beethoven arrived in Vienna in the late autumn of 1792, it was a city of perhaps two hundred thousand inhabitants. The capital of one of Europe's great dynasties, the Austro-Hungarian empire, the city ranked with London, Berlin and Paris as one of Europe's major metropolises. Then, as now, Vienna had a reputation for not taking itself too seriously, and for celebrating the most diverse forms of entertainment. Emperor Joseph II, a monarch deeply affected by Enlightenment ideals, had attempted a sweeping set of political reforms in the 1780s. After his death in 1790, however, these reforms were speedily overturned by his brothers Leopold and Franz, and by the first decades of the nineteenth century, Vienna was a virtual police state, with spies and secret informers everywhere. In fact, by taking a leadership role in the war against revolutionary France, Austria eventually became one of the most conservative states on the continent. However, at the time Beethoven arrived in the capital, perhaps because of the lingering effects of Joseph's reign, the city still retained some of its former light spirit.

Beethoven came to Vienna as a student, a member of the musical household of the Elector of Cologne on partial leave. It was fully assumed by the Elector and by Beethoven that he would soon return home. However, within a couple of years Beethoven was completely on his own, a freelance musician trying to make his way in the world. Ten years earlier, Mozart had attempted the same move in the same city, slipping the bonds that anchored him to the Archbishop of Salzburg, and had almost starved as a result. Musicians in the 1780s were expected to be attached to the households of great aristocratic families, where they were treated as servants, on a par with cooks and chambermaids. Even a Mozart could not challenge this system.

Things were a little different for Beethoven in the 1790s. A decade of social and philosophical change had put into question, if not ended, the old system of indentured servitude for musicians, although the aristocracy was still their primary source of employment. Perhaps a hundred noble families, numbering fewer than a thousand people, circumscribed the musical world that Ludwig van Beethoven entered in 1792. The public concert was still unknown in Vienna; it would be three years before any of the ordinary citizens of the city would have a chance to hear Beethoven play. Musical life took place in the private salons, theaters and opera houses of the elite, where upward of three hundred pianists vied for the attention and favors of the very rich. In any given week, Beethoven would attend five or six informal gatherings of musicians and their patrons. Some would be lavish concerts; most were intimate meetings of a few players and listeners, where new compositions would be debuted, old ones performed and, most importantly, players would improvise. The Viennese taste for instrumental music was the most advanced in the world, and their demand for both performers and composers of quality was insatiable.

Beethoven conquered this world first as a performer, and very soon after his arrival in Vienna. Armed with introductions from Count Waldstein and the patronage of the Elector back home, Beethoven gained easy access to the highest musical circles, where his impassioned playing and dazzling improvisation earned him instant acclaim. Soon this rough Rhinelander with his equally rough pianistic style became part of the musical scene, and eager patrons besieged him with invitations to perform at their soirées or teach their children.

From all reports, Beethoven was one of the greatest piano players of all time. Although his style was very wild and strong, especially compared with the more refined playing of his contemporaries, his ability to conjure up emotion and power on the keyboard was alternately fascinating and terrifying to his audiences. No pianist before him, except perhaps Mozart, had the ability to improvise so brilliantly. Beethoven would often play for more than an hour, making it all up as he went along, reducing his audiences to silence or tears. His performances of his own works, as they were composed, were equally thrilling.

One of the chief amusements of the Viennese public in the late eighteenth century was the staging of gruesome fights between animals in the local zoo. The aristocracy enjoyed their own version of this spectacle by setting up contests between their pianists. These were not the civilized competitions of today but exhausting battles, in which two performers, at two keyboards, would face each other sometimes for hours, each attempting to best his opponent by outplaying and outimprovising him. Beethoven never lost one of these encounters. Abbé Gelinek, a respected performer of an older school, hardly lasted a set with the young Beethoven: "That young man must be in league with the devil" was his parting remark. With Joseph Wölffl of Salzburg, the contest was more even — Beethoven's wild, impassioned playing contrasting sharply with Wölffl's delicate but extremely virtuosic performance. Daniel Steibelt, another famous pianist, was so thoroughly humiliated by Beethoven (who began a series of improvised variations by placing a Steibelt composition on the piano upside down and playing it with one finger) that he refused forever after to be in the same room with him.

Despite his dominance in these contests, Beethoven participated in them only reluctantly. His ambivalence regarding these soirées mirrored his feelings about the aristocracy; in general, Beethoven seems to have been both amused and bemused by his noble patrons. Although he clearly loved their company and enjoyed the entrée his art gave him into their glittering society, he keenly felt the truth of his position with them: he was not their friend or colleague but their plaything, a kind of musical court jester. It was a role he detested.

Beethoven used his increasing fame to fight against this humiliation. He would refuse to play on command if he was not in the mood. On one occasion a countess got down on her hands and knees to beg him to perform, precisely the kind of noble jest that infuriated him. He got up and left the room in a rage. Many was the time he would stop playing if he felt his audience was not properly attentive. "I will not play for such swine" was his comment as he exited one such gathering. If anything, this behavior endeared him even more completely to his aristocratic audiences. Perhaps they were amused by his "republican" displays, so fashionable in the early 1790s. He became celebrated as much for his temperament as for his playing.

Several patrons in particular "adopted" Beethoven: Prince Karl Lichnowsky, in whose home Beethoven lived for several years as a sort of permanent guest; Count Browne, an Irish-born notable; and Baron von Sweiten, a former champion of Mozart. These men and their families, influenced by Enlightenment values, treated Beethoven with an exaggerated regard. Lichnowsky instructed his servant that should he and Beethoven ever ring for him simultaneously, Beethoven should be the first served. Beethoven's frequent rudeness and lapses of taste were accepted with true noblesse oblige by his aristocratic patrons, who, following a pattern begun back in Bonn by Madame von Breuning, were prepared to indulge the occasional outburst from the talented young artist in return for the pleasure of hearing him play. Beethoven's personality, as well as his music, had begun to set the standard for musical artistry in the Austrian capital.

Beethoven's great successes first as a performer and then, after 1795, as a composer, helped lift the veil of sadness that had enveloped him for most of his first twenty years. He was beginning to taste the sweetness of life instead of its bitterness. The brighter world he had dimly glimpsed through the von Breunings, which had been denied him in Bonn, opened up to him in Vienna. Here Beethoven, now independent, began to create a life of his own. He surrounded himself with new friends, young men like himself, and took part in as many of the amusements of the city as he could. He took dancing lessons, bought a horse, and became something of a man about town. Years later, his biographers and friends would remark that this first decade in Vienna was perhaps the happiest period of Beethoven's life.

He himself was well aware of the change in his fortune and disposition. Just a year after his arrival in Vienna, in November of 1793, Beethoven wrote this letter to Eleonore von Breuning back in Bonn:

> With this you will receive a dedication from me to you concerning which I only wish that the work were a larger one and more worthy of you. . . . Take this trifle and remember that it comes from a friend who respects you greatly. . . . Let it be a reminder of the time when I spent so many and such blessed hours at your home. Perhaps it will keep me in your recollection, until I eventually return to you, which, it is true, is not likely to be soon, but oh, how we shall rejoice then, my dear friend. You will then find in your friend a happier man, one from whose visage time and a kindlier fate shall have smoothed out all the furrows of a hateful past.

It was in Vienna also that Beethoven's sexual energy seems to have found its first liberation. For a composer whose masculinity virtually shouts from every page, remarkably little is known about Beethoven's sexual life. He himself was reticent in its discussion, and his first biographers, Victorian to the core, almost completely suppressed this aspect of his nature. Although we know the names of several women with whom Beethoven was involved, the full canvas of his erotic life remains shrouded in darkness.

That the sexual was critical for Beethoven, however, can be inferred not merely by the energy pulsing through his music but by the comments of several of his earliest Viennese friends. Ferdinand Ries, an early pupil, remembers Beethoven turning to stare after beautiful women in the street, only to laugh guiltily when he realized Ries was observing him. Beethoven was often in love, according to Ries, who later commented, "When once I teased him about his conquest of a certain beautiful lady, he confessed that she had captivated him more intensely and longer than any other — seven whole months."

Franz Wegeler, Beethoven's boyhood friend who later joined him in Vienna, made similar observations:

Beethoven was never not in love and was usually involved to a high degree. . . . In Vienna, Beethoven was always involved in a love affair, at least as long as I lived there, and sometimes made conquests which could have been very difficult indeed, if not impossible, for many an Adonis.

If Beethoven behaved like a Greek god, he certainly did not look like one. Short, pock-marked, rude and unkempt, he did not cut the most attractive figure in Vienna, and often, if not always, the objects of his affection were either married or of a social standing far beyond his contemplation. The Enlightenment had not erased all the ancient distinctions between classes; Beethoven would suffer from the frustration of his humble upbringing all his life. Magdalena Willmann, a singer from Bonn, set a pattern when she supposedly refused Beethoven's offer of marriage in the mid-1790s in the firmest terms.

When asked why years later, she exclaimed, "Because he was so ugly, and half-crazy!"

Beethoven may not have been "half-crazy," but even in this happy period of his life, his personal eccentricities — apparent since boyhood — became more pronounced. He was a man with little control over his emotions and behavior, which may have made him an exciting artist but not an easy friend or acquaintance. Not only was he pugnacious and brittle with his patrons, he constantly managed to alienate even his closest associates. Always ready to believe the worst, Beethoven was forever taking precipitate action against his supposed enemies, for which he would later profusely apologize. Beethoven's biographers recount dozens of such incidents, some minor, some very serious. There was hardly a single friend he had not cut off for a time over some slight, real or imagined. Many of these estrangements would last months; some lasted years. And although Beethoven was aware of his fatal combination of poor judgment and extreme temper, he was unable to do much about it. What began as an eccentricity in the last decade of the eighteenth century would develop into a condition closely resembling paranoia in the first decades of the nineteenth.

Beethoven had originally expected to return home to Bonn after a few short months in the Austrian capital but soon abandoned those plans. Even when his father died just a few weeks after his arrival in Vienna — a macabre echo of the circumstances surrounding his mother's death five years earlier — Beethoven did not return home. When the Electorate of Cologne fell to conquering French Republican troops in 1794, a court that had survived for more than five hundred years disappeared overnight. Beethoven became a free citizen.

Beethoven's growing musical independence and maturity in Vienna led him inexorably to the career that would make his name throughout Europe: composition. However, if he had rather speedily joined the ranks of Vienna's top-ranking pianists, he was much more deliberate about the creative side of his art. Beethoven had come to Vienna to study composition with Haydn, but the lessons had proved less than a success. Beethoven needed more attention than Haydn was willing to provide, and so the young man began studying with other teachers in secret. After six months or so of this deception, his lessons with Haydn officially ended, although his studies continued for another two years. Beethoven was not a beginner when he arrived in Vienna but a musician of ten years' experience, yet he continued to work tirelessly at the rudiments of counterpoint and form, constantly seeking to improve his skills. All his life the passionate Beethoven — the man who could improvise for hours at a time — was studied, painstaking and deliberate as a composer. No other composer seems to have labored so long over his works, accumulating mounds of sketches and experimenting with countless approaches. Beethoven wrote a lot of music before he was done, but each composition was the result of long, hard effort.

His work paid off. His first few years in Vienna had been devoted to performing, but from about 1795 onward he became equally well known as a composer. Slowly and steadily a major body of work appeared from his pen. As his confidence increased, more and more of his energy was consumed by composing.

These first-period works (basically the music Beethoven wrote before 1800) present an interesting mixture of the new and the old. Although Beethoven would become one of the most revolutionary composers in music history, he was very careful in his approach to his art. As one commentator has noted, it was as though Beethoven wanted to be sure of the old rules of composition before he broke them all. Most of these early works took on the form and much of the language of Beethoven's illustrious predecessors, especially Mozart and Haydn.

Yet despite the conservatism of these early works (at least judged by the standards of his later compositions), the originality of Beethoven's voice was unmistakable. It was an urgent and rough voice, blending a rich musical imagination with a daring approach to technique. Although Beethoven had his enthusiastic admirers, his work was not universally applauded, even in these early years. Haydn, his teacher, was always of two minds about his pupil, admiring the skill in his composition but ambivalent about the character of the voice.

Beethoven tasted his first successes as a composer with his chamber works, his Septet, op. 20, Quintet, op. 5, and opus 1 trios. These intimate groupings of wind and string instruments were great favorites with the aristocratic audiences of the late eighteenth century, and Beethoven used them to test his growing compositional skill. But his most daring and engaging music was reserved for the piano. Beethoven was a master pianist, after all, and understood the instrument as did few others. He could immediately perform everything he wrote as well as sell the publishing rights to supplement his income. The three opus 2 sonatas, dedicated to Haydn, were published in 1795; his next, op. 7, in 1796.

These early piano sonatas marked Beethoven as a composer eager to experiment with musical form and language and anxious to develop his own voice. They were the vehicles by which Beethoven began to express the combination of power, success and confidence that marked his first years in Vienna, his first real attempts at musical self-expression. They are also based on a formal plan that Beethoven borrowed from tradition but imbued with his own distinctive personality: sonata form. Sonata form galvanized Beethoven's work as a composer, providing him a basic musical organization that he used all his artistic life. It was a form that allowed his passion and originality to be structured within clear, if flexible, bounds. It is an essential key to understanding his musical universe. So we'll turn our attention to the first piano sonata he ever wrote, op. 2, no. 1, and its special organization.

6

The Eternal Guide:
Sonata Form

If *Au clair de la lune* is a single-celled artistic life form and *Für Elise* a simple primate, Beethoven's op. 2, no. 1 is a fully developed musical *Homo sapiens*, an example of sonata form, one of the most fascinating organizational complexes musicians have ever developed.

Originally *sonata* simply meant a piece that was played on instruments rather than sung by the human voice. For a long time in Western musical history, all music was vocal, and its form depended almost entirely on the texts on which the music was based. As a setting either of the Mass or of a poem, the design of the music was dictated by the design of the words. However, in the century or so before Beethoven was born, instrumental music began to achieve growing independence and popularity. More and more effort was expended on composing for purely instrumental forces.

Composers are like other inventors, constantly seeking improvements in their art's power and efficiency. So several generations of composers kept tinkering away in their artistic basements with the form of instrumental composition. For several decades, experimentation became the rule. However, by the time Beethoven reached musical maturity, in the mid-1780s, sonata form had come to dominate the writing of most serious instrumental music.

Sonata form had begun to develop in the mid-eighteenth century as a reaction to the severe contrapuntal forms — both vocal and instrumental — that had been the basis of music for centuries. In a Europe starting to shake off the religious determinism that had shaped social life for close to a millennium, a new kind of music was needed, one that could give voice to the secular and rational forces sweeping the continent. The sonata thus became a microcosm of changing social mores, a musical play complete with characters (individual musical ideas) and a plot (their organization). Developed over many decades by dozens of composers, sonata form was eventually perfected by Haydn and Mozart a decade or so before Beethoven began his serious work as a composer.

Sonata form was Beethoven's great musical obsession. Apart from his single opera and some occasional music, Beethoven entrusted all of his musical ideas to this form. All his symphonies, concertos, string quartets, violin sonatas, piano sonatas and most of his wind music were organized according to this plan. Although Beethoven went through at least two major musical metamorphoses in his career, he stuck with sonata form all his life. His first piano sonata, written in 1795, may have little in common emotionally with his last, written in 1822, but both are based on the same organization. Learning to hear sonata form is thus the key to appreciating virtually every composition Beethoven wrote.

All creators need frameworks on which to hang their ideas. Without them, their spontaneous bursts of creativity would be chaotic and largely unintelligible. Deciding in advance the general shape of a work can be a great aid to creativity and imaginative thinking.

It is also more than that. Choosing the right form is a crucial part of the artistic process, because the form of a work can have profound effects on its meaning. It is more than just a means to an end; it is a kind of end in itself. A real form incorporates simple but fundamental ideas that strike profound emotional resonances within us, and any work organized by that form's principles will share those resonances. In architecture, a dome is a good example. It doesn't really matter whether the dome sits atop St. Peter's Basilica or a baseball stadium, the psychological meaning and power of the shape works the same way. Any architect choosing to use a dome in a building will be able to share in that power of enclosure and harmony. What is true of the dome in architecture is also true of the sonata in music: it is based on a fundamental psychological principle.

For a sonata, that overriding principle is the idea of return. In sonata form, a musical idea or mood is established in a work, then abandoned, then reestablished. This *aba* pattern, as simple as it seems, is the organizing spark of music as graceful as a Mozart piano concerto or as powerful as Beethoven's Ninth Symphony. It became an extremely important tool for composers determined to put into purely instrumental music the widest range of dramatic and artistic possibilities. This simple organization allowed music to enter into new spiritual worlds.

The reason for this is that the idea of return is a central emotional response in human consciousness. Think of all the myths and stories that are based on this idea, from the *Odyssey* to *The Wizard of Oz*. To humans, being lost, being away from home, is terrifying: the return home is thus always joyful. As reconciliation, fulfillment or simply eternal process, the idea of return expresses deep psychological needs. On a spiritual level, it is the idea that lies at the heart of most religious belief: the reunification of the individual with his or her God.

Until sonata form was developed, the closest a composer could hope to get to this central emotional reality was by setting to music texts that described it. With sonata form it became possible to tap into the notion of return without using words, bringing music's deep power of representation into the service of a profound psychological idea.

The sonata principle was applied to several levels of the music it organized. First, it determined the order of the different sections, or movements, that made up a sonata-based work — which could be a concerto, symphony or string quartet as well as a work called a sonata. Second, it provided the key to the design of the first movement of those works. Keep this in mind as you read this book and listen to Beethoven's music. From here on, every work we look at will be organized in sonata form.

In its large sense, sonata form brought a certain discipline into what in the sixteenth and seventeenth centuries had been a relatively arbitrary arrangement of sections in musical works. Before the sonata, longer works were often made up of a series of dances, with not a great deal of thought going into their order. Under the influence of the sonata principle, this began to change: sonatas were almost always written in three or four movements (something like acts in a play), whose character and relationship to one another became fixed.

The most important movement of a sonata is the first, usually played in a quick tempo (*allegro* in Italian). This movement sets the emotional character of the whole work and provides its main musical motifs. It is the "home" section of large-scale sonata form. A sonata's first movement is followed by one or two contrasting movements, representing the "away" concept. The second movement is usually slow and contemplative; the third, often a light-hearted minuet and trio, a holdover from the earlier era's dance movements. Finally, the last movement reestablishes something of the mood of the opening, usually in the same key as the first movement and almost always again at a faster tempo. However, the final movement of a sonata is generally lighter than the first, providing a joyous, sunnier return "home" after the night of the middle movements.

Thousands of symphonies, sonatas and concertos were written in the eighteenth and nineteenth centuries according to this outline. It became something of a convention, a basic musical form. Composers began to plan their compositions and organize their musical thoughts according to its demands. They could determine in advance the kinds of musical ideas they would need for each of the form's sections. They could and did stockpile musical ideas.

However, the sonata principle would be somewhat limited if it only determined the order of movements in an instrumental composition. The genius of the sonata principle is that it sets its stamp far more completely. Like a set of Russian nesting dolls, the sonata principle organizes all aspects of a work, from the large-scale structure of movements to the set-up of individual movements and of the smaller sections within those movements. No more complete musical form has ever been invented.

Perhaps the most significant use of sonata form was in its organization of individual movements within a larger sonata structure. The first movement of a sonata was almost always organized in this manner, and often one of the other movements as well. The use of this pattern became so widespread that certain technical terms were invented to describe its various sections. Generally it's a good idea to steer clear of musical jargon, but these terms are actually useful. If they didn't exist, we'd have to invent them.

The first *a* ("home") section in a sonata movement is called the *exposition*, because in it the main musical ideas of the movement are "exposed." The *b* ("away") section is the *development*, since the musical ideas are developed within it; and the third section, the second *a*, is the recapitulation, the return of the main ideas.

Sonata form is more tightly focused than the sectional form by which a piece like *Für Elise* is organized. We certainly had an *a* section in that work — the main idea that kept returning — but neither of the other two ideas in the work could be called a development of that idea. They simply followed it, without much fuss. The musical ideas in a sonata are more closely linked; they influence one another, shape one another, transform one another. Although the musical statements themselves are often exactly like the ideas we heard in *Für Elise*, their relationships are more complex.

Here, then, in its simplest form, is how a sonata movement is laid out:

A Exposition
B Development
A Recapitulation

The exposition section begins the movement, laying out its main musical ideas and setting its character, just as in *Für Elise*. However, in a sonata, the exposition is generally made up of more than one musical idea and is usually repeated, so that an audience can get those ideas firmly implanted in their minds. In the development section, those ideas are transformed and varied into whatever shape a composer's imagination can invent. The development section is the most unpredictable part of a sonata movement, where mystery and surprise dominate. Finally, with the recapitulation, the suspense of the development gives way to the return of the familiar exposition section, often replayed virtually note for note.

The exposition-development-recapitulation pattern of a first movement in a sonata may be the most significant application of the sonata principle in classical music, but its influence does not end there. The *aba* pattern also organizes the movement's exposition and recapitulation. Not one but two main ideas are presented in an exposition. The first begins the piece and acts as the main musical motif for the entire movement. The second is introduced, in a different key, to contrast with the first. Often the first returns, in a section called the coda, which ties off the exposition and prepares for the development. The recapitulation repeats these three sections, although the middle section stays in the same key as the first and third. A complete diagram of sonata form therefore looks like this:

A First Movement (fast — allegro)

A Exposition
- a First Theme (tonic — home key)
- b Second theme (new key)
- a Coda

B Development

A Recapitulation
- a First Theme (home key)
- b Second Theme (home key)
- a Coda

B Second and sometimes third movements (slow)

A Finale (fast)

Sonata form may look like just a simple diagram at this moment, but when you've heard the breadth of music that was based on its design, you will marvel at its flexibility and power. Sonata form allowed instrumental music to make lengthy, coherent statements, in movements that last ten minutes or more and pieces that last thirty or more. Considering that the average musical idea takes no more than a few seconds to play, organization on that scale is a significant aesthetic achievement.

Originally, during the Age of Reason, sonata form was valued for the perfect symmetry of its design. Sonata form is a triumph of balance. First and last movements are balanced by two middle, contrasting ones. Exposition and recapitulation, often made up of exactly the same musical material, similarly balance perfectly on the fulcrum of the development. For much of Haydn's and Mozart's lifetimes and a small portion of Beethoven's, this sense of balance was sonata form's most significant feature.

It was not to remain so. Beethoven progressively unleashed the dramatic possibilities of sonata form, overwhelming its neat symmetry. He was the first composer to bring to the notion of return inherent in sonata form a sense of fulfillment, emotional release and revelation. Balance and symmetry may have been acceptable aesthetic values in the sophisticated salons of the late eighteenth century, the world into which Beethoven was born. But during his lifetime, the drama of revolution demanded a different theme from its artists. It was Beethoven's genius to recognize that the new accents of music could still be expressed within the old forms. More than any other composer, Beethoven exploited the symbolic possibilities of sonata form, the way its musical organization mirrors fundamental emotional realities. Most significantly, the emergence of the exposition into the sunlight of the recapitulation after the darkness of the development could be given profound psychological significance. Within the symmetry of Mozart's and Haydn's form lay a nucleus of powerful emotion. Beethoven's entire artistic mission was to split the atom of the sonata and liberate the power it contained.

The seeds of the future Beethoven were all present in his first set of sonatas, opus 2. Hearing the design in these works will prepare the ground for you to appreciate all the works of his maturity. The form of the sonata unites and animates them all.

7

Op. 2, No. 1:
The First Sonata

Beethoven gave opus numbers, the sign of musical respectability and significance, to thirty-two piano sonatas. The first three — gathered together as opus 2 — were written around 1795; the last one — opus 111 — in 1822. Among the thirty-two are some of the best-known pieces of music ever composed: the *Moonlight* Sonata, the *Pathétique*, the *Appassionata*, the *Waldstein*, the *Hammerklavier*. Beethoven was first and foremost a pianist, and he gave to the piano some of his most important musical thoughts. Next to his symphonies, Beethoven's piano works represent his most powerful statements.

With all the musical treasures contained in the later piano sonatas, it is easy to ignore the earlier ones, or to see them only as curiosities, the first creations of what was to become the greatest musical mind of a generation.

But this would be a mistake. These early sonatas are important, because Beethoven used them to experiment with the musical ideas that later found their way into his symphonies, string quartets and concertos. If these works still retain a trace of the courtly style of the late eighteenth century, they are, nevertheless, undeniably Beethoven. And because they are a little less intricate than his later works, they make a good place to start investigating Beethoven's use of sonata form.

As you prepare to listen to the first movement of op. 2, no. 1, remind yourself of the basic pattern of sonata form (see diagram on page 51). And think back to *Für Elise*. The most significant difference between that short piece and this sonata movement is the complexity of the sonata's musical ideas. There are more of them, and their relationships to each other are more intricate. However, the basic language is identical. If you could follow the sequence of ideas in *Für Elise*, you'll be able to do the same in op. 2, no. 1. Once again, listen to the CD as you read along, pause button at the ready.

Just as in *Für Elise*, in the sonata the most important music is the first you hear. The opening musical idea provides the character of the work, its mood, its energy level — everything that is central to its artistic meaning. However, in a sonata, that first idea takes on another important function. The return of the opening idea almost always signals the beginning of a new section in the design. The main theme begins the exposition; a revision of it usually begins the development; its return always signals the start of the recapitulation. Composers reserved the main theme for these key moments. If you were to hear it too many other times, you would soon get confused, and the formal logic of the work would falter. Keep listening for this main theme; when you hear it return, something important is happening in the music.

Like so many themes Beethoven used in his work, the main idea of op. 2, no. 1 is very straightforward. A broken chord is played in the right hand, one note after the other, rising through an octave and a half and ending with a little flourish, called a turn. Rhythmically, the idea is very simple: five single notes of equal value, followed by a triplet turn. Melodically, it is equally plain, outlining a basic triad finished off with a little ornamental tag.

Beethoven makes the most of this musical motif. He repeats it immediately, but this time with four single notes leading to the turn. He then extracts just the second half of the idea and repeats it twice, until he finally finishes off the phrase with a broken chord reminiscent of the opening single notes.

Listen to this first phrase a couple of times. It goes by quickly and seems very simple, but it contains a lot of artistry. Notice how the progressive shortening of the idea builds a sense of urgency. In only eight bars Beethoven has created a strong forward push, one of the defining characteristics of his music. This sense of forward motion is critical in sonata form. As listeners, we must always be moving ahead, anticipating the next section, wondering what's going to happen next. As soon as our musical interest flags, the propelling force of the form dissipates, and the drama inherent in it is lost.

Beethoven keeps the engine running in op. 2, no. 1 by giving us a second version of the theme immediately, only this time starting the idea five notes lower and in the left hand. But Beethoven doesn't repeat his idea note for note. After beginning the same way, he starts to play around with the idea, especially that little turn in its second half. Four times it is repeated just by itself, with a different harmonic background each time, keeping the spirit of the first idea alive without repeating it exactly. This splitting of musical ideas into smaller components and then treating the components as independent ideas is another of Beethoven's basic compositional techniques. It allows him to link musical sections through repetition without fatiguing his audiences. It gives to his works a sense of musical logic, a compelling sense of connectedness.

However, Beethoven also knew when he had exhausted an idea and should move on, as he does here. After this play with the turn, he introduces a short transition section, a little four-note tune heard three times, twice in single notes in the right hand, then doubled in octaves. Beethoven elides this transition idea with the main theme that precedes it, so you don't have a lot of warning that it's coming.

However, it's important to register these transition phrases, as they have a vital part to play in the overall organization. Because sonata form is a musical organism that constantly moves from one idea to another, the bridges between them are critical parts of the design, not mere interludes between the "good" stuff of the themes. Beethoven took considerable care with transitions; if they could not keep listeners' interest alive, the work's momentum would flag. They also serve as an early-warning system signaling that the music is about to move into a new formal section.

In op. 2, no. 1, the transition section leads almost imperceptibly to a new musical idea, starting on a little roughness of a dissonance in the right hand and accompanied by a rolling bass in the left. (Often a change in the accompaniment tips you off to a new musical idea in a sonata.) Where the first idea in the piece ascended the scale, this one descends and adds a little skip upward at its finale. With this phrase, the exposition has moved from its first, *a* section to its second, *b* section.

Picking out the transition to the second theme in a sonata exposition is often tricky, even for seasoned listeners. The first theme is no problem; it's almost always the music that starts the piece. But the second theme, that's harder. It comes at you in the midst of other musical ideas, sometimes announced clearly, sometimes less clearly. How do you know which of the bits of music you hear is really the second theme? It's important for you to register this theme; otherwise the *aba* pattern of the exposition will lose some of its effect.

Composers used the same techniques in creating a second theme as they did for a first. A phrase will appear with an identifiable rhythm or melody and will be given a certain prominence through repetition. As well, the second theme will usually have a different character from the first to reinforce the change. Remember the second theme (idea) of *Für Elise* and the lengths Beethoven went to to differentiate it from the first.

Beethoven is a little more mischievous in this sonata and stretches, if not breaks, one of the form's conventions. The second theme is introduced very abruptly here, almost sounding like an extension of the transition idea that precedes it. Usually, a transition section is longer to prepare listeners for an impending change in the music. As well, the second theme here does not represent that complete a change from the first, musically or emotionally. The theme itself is a mirror image of the first, descending rather than ascending, and its mood is similar. How can we be sure this is the second theme at all?

It is the amount of time Beethoven devotes to this musical idea that is the tip-off to its structural importance. A thematic section will be relatively substantial in length; a mere episode will come and go in a few bars. So Beethoven repeats this new thematic idea three complete times, note for note, to ensure that you register it in your consciousness, before extending it with a little passage in the right hand that completes the *b* section of the exposition. Notice that the rolling bass in the left hand continues throughout this entire second section.

That rolling bass gives way to a second transition section (which again begins almost before we notice it), characterized by a long descending scale passage in the right hand, repeated twice. Finally, the brief coda of the exposition makes its appearance, beginning with a leap upward that is actually a quote from one of the early bars of the first-theme section of the sonata. This clever allusion to the sonata's main idea allows Beethoven to suggest a repeat without actually providing one, and helps him frame the second idea in the exposition with two versions of the first, the *aba* pattern. Symmetry and drama have been equally well served. The coda theme is repeated three times before the exposition comes to a close on two big chords.

I would suggest you listen to the exposition again because of its crucial importance to the entire movement, but I don't have to, because it is repeated, note for note, in the score. The exposition was almost always played twice in sonata form to allow audiences a second chance to hear its main ideas before entering the wilds of the development. During the repeat, concentrate on the first and second themes and the relationship between them. When he gets to the development, Beethoven is going to assume you're familiar with them.

As well, when you listen to the exposition a second time, you may notice something else: it ends in a different key than it began. While the sonata opened with a minor, sadder-sounding key, it ends on a brighter-sounding major chord. Harmony and changes of harmony — the choice of chords to accompany a melody and the movement from one set of chords to another — are among the most powerful components of music, but are also the most subliminal. We don't normally notice the subtle changes in harmony that accompany the development of a piece of music, and to point them out away from a piano keyboard can be difficult. However, you should know that harmonic design was very dear to classical composers, and the sonata principle affected a piece's harmonies as much as any other component. The movement of harmony from one key to another and then back was a major feature of sonata form, for some commentators the most significant home-away-home relationship in the piece.

The first theme of the exposition was always played in the home key; generally a new key was used for the second theme and retained for the rest of the exposition. Anything might happen harmonically during the development, but the recapitulation always marked the return not just of the exposition's main idea but of its key as well. That home key was maintained throughout the recapitulation so the movement could end with the same harmony with which it began — the sonata story told in harmonic terms.

Harmonic change was most important to the development section of a sonata movement, the adventure away from the home territory outlined by the exposition. Stepping into the development of a sonata is like boarding a ship for a sea journey. You know where you are, and you know where you're headed, but the journey itself is a mystery; anything might happen before you see familiar shores again. And it doesn't matter how often you've taken the journey before, that mixture of anticipation and anxiety is still there.

The development section of a sonata may have begun as an exercise in symmetry, a temporary diversion to enhance the experience of balance between the first and third sections. However, over time it became the most important section of sonata form. As drama supplanted balance as a musical goal, the potential of the development section to surprise, move and intensify the musical experience was consistently exploited. If the power of the third section of sonata form — the return — was to be most keenly felt, listeners had to experience a perilous musical trip to get there.

You might think that the easiest way to provide contrast in the development would be to compose brand-new music for it, with a new theme and a new character, something completely different from the exposition. There are developments like that, but they are the exceptions. Instead, classical composers made a surprising discovery. The development section — the away section — was in fact more powerful when it used material already introduced in the exposition but presented in new melodic and harmonic combinations. To hear the familiar in unfamiliar surroundings was more affecting than to hear something brand new.

The development section thus became a source of new meanings for old musical ideas — a sort of dream world where musical objects seen clearly and safely in the light of the exposition now moved in new, surprising relationships. This sense of musical otherness eventually became the sonata's most powerful moment, especially in Beethoven's hands.

The development of op. 2, no. 1 does not fully exploit that potential (it would take Beethoven another decade or so before he himself understood the full dramatic implications of the development), but it does provide an idea of how development sections are put together.

Beethoven begins the development by quoting the main theme, always a sign that a new section is beginning. However, this time the theme is not in F minor, the original key, but in A-flat major, the key in which the coda ended. Note how different the music sounds with its new harmony. Beethoven could have started the development anywhere, since there are virtually no rules for development sections. But to hear the main theme now in a major key gives us a sense of the familiar and the new at the same time.

Beethoven merely quotes a bit of the main theme to begin the development, compressing it from the original by adding the turn figure twice in a row. He presents this a second time, harmonies changing in the left hand, and then — boom! — plunges us immediately into a version of the second theme. A transition that took twelve bars in the exposition is accomplished with a single note in the development. Even if you've heard this piece dozens of times, the abruptness of that transition takes you by surprise. This is what development sections are all about. The measured balance of the exposition is torn apart: musical ideas are butted up against one another in new keys or new combinations, sometimes only appearing for an instant, sometimes being prolonged past their expected time. We never know what to expect; musical tension is at its highest.

Beethoven was a master in the art of musical suspense. In an instant he plunges us into the second theme in the development, but then is in no hurry to leave the idea. He plays the theme through exactly as it appeared in the exposition, all three times, even including the little extension in the right hand. However, the last three notes of that extension are radically altered from the original to allow Beethoven to repeat the theme in a different and unexpected key. Listen for this change of harmony. It creates a remarkable sense of disturbance in the music. All of a sudden, even though we are listening to a familiar theme, we realize we have no idea what is coming next in the music. We are completely in Beethoven's hands.

After the change in harmony, the second theme begins a second time as though it were going to continue through its complete cycle, but Beethoven varies it yet again. The theme is played twice through in the right hand, as expected, but then the hands switch places, and the theme is heard in the bass. Three times the second theme is heard in the lower register, each time beginning on a different note, each time with a different set of harmonies. The regularly changing harmonies (one per bar) give the music the sensation of moving faster than it actually does, as our ears must constantly readjust (if only subconsciously) to register the music's changing harmonic framework.

Having speeded up our internal musical clock, Beethoven then proceeds to reverse the effect. The constantly moving second-theme bass line gives way to a series of accented notes in both treble and bass, which stretches the harmonies and melodies of the music. It's almost as though Beethoven has temporarily moved the piece into slow motion.

The lull in the action is purposeful. Beethoven is about to build to the climax of the development and needs a more neutral section to provide its starting point. The left hand recommences its rolling figure, now sounding more ominous because more exposed than before. On top of it, Beethoven plays several two-note figures, actually the first two notes of the second theme, now widely separated from one another by half a bar of silence. The tension mounts. Beethoven repeats the idea, turning the two-note figure into a three-note figure, then doubles the idea in octaves and moves the repetition of the figure closer and closer together. This is musical acceleration, a technique of which Beethoven was a master. Without changing the basic pulse of the music, he can make it sound as though it's going faster and faster, increasing the musical excitement to build to a tremendous climax.

Except that in the case of this sonata, the climax never comes. At precisely the point where you expect the music to reach a crescendo, Beethoven, ever the master of musical surprise, reduces the texture to an unexpected single repeated note, played as softly as possible. Beethoven loved this technique; he used it in several of his most famous compositions. A single note is the most neutral and most malleable device in music. It can move anywhere and do anything, thus allowing a composer the most perfect flexibility. It takes courage to expect an audience to listen to a single tolling note for any length of time, but it's a gamble that usually pays off.

Beethoven turns his single repeated note into a two-note chord and then provides us with the last surprise of the development section: the little turn from the first theme of the movement, now played just by itself. We had been spending so much time with the second theme in the development, we had completely forgotten the first. By quoting just this tag end of that original idea, Beethoven can remind us of it in the simplest of ways. The turn is repeated half a dozen times as the harmony moves with it, preparing us for the reintroduction of our home key and our home idea. The recap has begun.

The development of the first movement of op. 2, no. 1 is only fifty-two bars long. Within a decade Beethoven would be writing development sections two and three times its length. However, the op. 2 development gives you an idea of what is possible with this section. Surprise and mystery are its keynotes, cleverness and creativity its characteristics.

There is always a sense of relief at the beginning of the recapitulation in sonata form. We have been presented with a series of unpredictable musical ideas in the development, never exactly sure what was coming next. How nice to bask in the familiar sunshine of the movement's main idea, secure in the knowledge that the rough weather of the development has passed.

Because the point of the recapitulation was to reestablish a sense of musical security, composers deviated at their peril from the pattern set in their expositions. The idea was to build a section that symmetrically balanced the exposition by making it sound as much like the opening section as possible.

With one exception. Remember that to accentuate the sonata principle, the second theme in the exposition was played in a different key than the first. In the recap, however, everything is written in the home key, first and second theme both. Because the format is otherwise identical to the exposition, a few changes are needed in the recap to recast it all in the home key. However, composers tried to keep these changes to a minimum.

When you listen to the recap of op. 2, no. 1, you might be able to pick out the few added notes here or extra bar there that enable Beethoven to reshape the entire recap in F minor. Occasionally, he even has to change register (the location of the hands on the keyboard). Still, the overwhelming impression is one of identity, not of difference, between the recap and the exposition. Recapitulations existed to provide a balance for the exposition, and as close a balance as possible. Even at his most radical, Beethoven tinkered very little with his recaps, as is the case here. Other than the harmonic changes noted above, the recapitulation is an exact model of the exposition. Themes appear in the same place and occupy the same length of time; transition passages appear as in the exposition. Nothing is foreshortened, nothing left out. Only at the very end is a series of extra chords added to provide a satisfying finish to the movement. The trials of the development are redeemed by the security and satisfaction of this musical return home. The third part of the *aba* sonata pattern has fallen into place.

Depending on the recording or performance you listen to, you might hear something a little different at the end of the recapitulation of op. 2, no. 1. In the original score, Beethoven marked a repeat of both the development and the recapitulation (probably to balance off the repeat of the exposition), although not every pianist observes it.

If your recording does, you will hear the development start again after the movement seems to come to an end. This repeated second half of a sonata movement was not unusual in the mid-eighteenth century, but it was a technique Beethoven very rarely used again after this sonata. It's not hard to see why.

A return to the away section of the development after the satisfying arrival home in the recapitulation makes little psychological or musical sense. In an earlier era, when developments were less dramatic and the sense of journey in a sonata movement less pronounced, such a repeat would not offend. But here it sounds like a mistake, and in Beethoven's developing world it was a mistake. It is an exception to the sonata pattern that definitely proves the rule. Once you have returned home in the recapitulation of a sonata, the psychological circle of the movement has been closed. It should not be reopened.

Despite this one anomaly, the first movement of op. 2, no. 1 is a good example of sonata form. Beethoven has clearly and simply outlined its main architectural features and demonstrated its dramatic possibilities. As well, basic features of his musical language are in evidence: the simple, unadorned themes; the use of dissonant, almost ugly musical sounds; the emphasis on drama and surprise rather than on beauty and charm to make a musical point. These were the elements Beethoven used to create his potent musical style, by turning roughness into energy and power. What he first experimented with in these early sonatas became the groundwork for his later achievements.

Along with the rest of the music Beethoven was composing in the last five years of the eighteenth century, the three sonatas of opus 2 are a portrait of a young composer testing his art, eager for the challenges that lay ahead. His personal and professional life seemed on a solid footing for the first time ever. Yet, within a very few years, Beethoven would be confronted by a desperate crisis that threatened to shatter his world. In the last few months of 1799, when he was only twenty-nine, Beethoven noticed that he was beginning to go deaf.

8

"Speak Louder, Shout, for I Am Deaf"

As the eighteenth century gave birth to the nineteenth, Beethoven was beginning what looked to be a wonderful career. His music was taking on new assurance; he was the center of an increasingly large coterie of friends and admirers; publishers competed with one another to purchase his works. As he wrote to Eleonore von Breuning, he was one for whom "time . . . had smoothed out the furrows of a hateful past." He looked to the future with excited confidence.

Yet within two years, according to his own testimony, Beethoven had considered suicide and had resigned himself to a "wretched existence," cursing his fate and confronting a life of interminable loneliness and sorrow, broken only by the joys of his creative activity. The world knows now what few of his contemporaries suspected in those years: Beethoven, one of the most famous musicians of his time, was going deaf.

Beethoven's deafness is one of the most incredible facets of an already extraordinary life. That so gifted a musician, of all those around him, should be afflicted with loss of hearing, seems perversely cruel, an ironic calculation of fate. But Beethoven's response to his deafness became as significant to his life and to his career as the disease itself. At first despairing at the possible loss of his profession and his art, Beethoven eventually determined to "grab Fate by the throat," as he put it, and carry on. Beethoven had overcome demons before, but this adversary was more tenacious. Yet his steadfast resolve to deny the destructive potential of his disability liberated in him a power which, when translated into music, produced sounds that still thrill the world today.

Beethoven first noticed he was having trouble with his hearing in the late 1790s. Initially, he paid little attention to these small difficulties, too busy with work and fired with ambition to worry about what must have seemed to him an impossibility — that his hearing, his "most noble faculty," as he called it, was deteriorating. However, by the end of 1800, Beethoven's uneasiness had turned first to concern, then to panic. By that time, he suffered from a continual buzzing in his ears, was having trouble hearing high frequencies and found it difficult to follow normal conversations; at the same time, loud noises caused him severe pain. Today we know that these symptoms are consistent with deterioration of the auditory nerve, although this diagnosis was not made in Beethoven's lifetime and could only be confirmed after his death.

The cause of the deterioration remains a mystery. In Beethoven's day, everything from a sharp fall to the ground he suffered in 1795 to problems with his bowels was confidently brought forward as the source of his affliction. Today, complications due to syphilis have been added to the list. For all the speculation, no one really knows.

As fears of total deafness began to haunt Beethoven, he consulted physician after physician, eagerly applying their remedies, living on the upward draft of his hopes for a cure, always to be plunged downward when such hopes evaporated. When one doctor's treatment proved ineffectual, a new doctor would be found and a new remedy tried. New hopes would be created, new disappointments felt. Beethoven was subjected to a series of treatments, common for the day, which probably worsened, rather than improved, his condition. Cold baths were recommended, then warm baths; a tree bark plaster was applied to his arms (quite painfully, it seems), cotton swabs inserted into his ears. Nothing worked. Beethoven's hearing continued its progressive decline.

From this time onward, his deafness would become the chief emotional and psychological fact of Beethoven's life, the point at which his art and his life most painfully converged. Whether as a fate to be overcome, a condition to be disguised and concealed, or an impediment to his musical career, deafness became the composer's central reality.

A deaf musician seems an impossible contradiction, an oxymoron. And Beethoven's deafness did exact a tremendous toll on him, yet, surprisingly, more on the personal than on the professional level. For one thing, the deterioration in Beethoven's hearing, although progressive and unalterable, was gradual, and there were lengthy periods when it seems to have stabilized. As late as 1806, a friend who lived in the same building had not noticed his affliction. Beethoven faced no real restriction on his performing career until around 1810, when he was forced to give up solo recitals. However, he was able to participate in chamber concerts for a few years after that.

It was only after 1814 that his deafness became an insurmountable problem for him as a performer; by 1817 he could not hear music at all. Although some hearing persisted in his left ear until his death, for all intents and purposes, Beethoven was completely deaf for the last decade of his life. Still, as inexorable as his slide into aural darkness was, Beethoven was able to work as a practicing musician for almost thirty years, a longer career than that enjoyed by many healthy musicians — Mozart, to name one.

As well, as fantastic as it might seem, it is possible to compose music without hearing it, so that Beethoven's deafness never seriously impeded his compositional labors; he continued to compose right up to the last year of his life. All of Beethoven's most significant compositions were written after his hearing began to desert him. Some of his greatest, such as the *Missa Solemnis* and the Ninth Symphony, were composed after he had gone completely deaf, within an inner chamber of complete silence.

How is this possible? Before he lost his hearing completely, Beethoven had spent every day for close to forty years in constant contact with music and musical combinations. They had become internalized for him, as they have for many other musicians. Because musicians spend the greater part of their lives using notes and chords the way the rest of us use words, they possess the same ability to compose music in their heads as we all have in composing words and sentences, without immediately having to write them down or hear them. A deaf playwright could continue to write works for the stage even though he or she was not able to hear actors actually speaking lines. The words would be heard where they counted, in the artist's imagination. A deaf composer works in the same way.

None of this is to imply that Beethoven's impairment was of no concern to him as a professional musician. Anxiety over his hearing overwhelmed him the moment he recognized his symptoms, long before anyone else had the slightest notion of his difficulties. For years he lived in constant terror that his condition might be discovered and that he would be subject to ridicule or humiliation in Vienna's competitive musical society. And his last decade of total deafness was terrible. In 1816, he began to use ear trumpets to little effect. By 1818, all discourse with Beethoven took place by way of little "Conversation Books," which he carried with him everywhere. His few attempts to play or conduct in his last years were tragic disasters.

However, it was in the social and human sphere, not the musical, that Beethoven's deafness was most devastating. Modern research has confirmed that deafness is the most socially isolating of all the diseases of the senses. Sound is the most ubiquitous of sensations, surrounding us with an aural blanket of security. To lose that and be imprisoned in the solitary confinement of deafness can be a harrowing experience, in which simple social intercourse becomes impossible and even terrifying. Deprived of our ability to converse with our neighbors, we can become wary of them, and withdraw.

Intentionally or not, Beethoven followed this pattern. He had been a difficult and solitary individual at the best of times, and his infirmity intensified these natural inclinations. To hide his affliction, he began to avoid the company of others. More and more, he retreated into his own private world, increasingly unhappy and alone.

In the beginning, there were few in Vienna to whom Beethoven dared confide his situation, but two friends outside the city — Karl Amenda and Franz Wegeler — both received letters from Beethoven in 1801 describing his problems. To Amenda he wrote:

> Your Beethoven is living an unhappy life, quarreling with nature and its creator, often cursing the latter for surrendering his creatures to the merest accident which often breaks or destroys the most beautiful blossoms. Know that my noblest faculty, my hearing, has greatly deteriorated. When you were still with me I felt the symptoms but kept silent; now it is continually growing worse, and whether or not a cure is possible has become a question. How sad is my lot, I must avoid all things that are dear to me and what is more must live among such miserable and egotistical people. . . . Oh, how happy I should be if my hearing were completely restored, then I would hurry to you. However, as it is I must stay away from everything and the most beautiful years of my life must pass by without my accomplishing all that my talent and powers bid me do — A sad resignation must be my refuge, although, indeed, I am resolved to rise above every obstacle.

Many of the same sentiments are contained in his letter to Wegeler:

> I can truly say that I am living a wretched life. For two years I have avoided almost all social gatherings because it is impossible for me to say to people "I am deaf." If I belonged to any other profession it would be easier, but in my profession it is a frightful state. Then there are my enemies, who are numerous, what would they say about this? . . . If possible I will bid defiance to my fate, although there will be moments in my life when I shall be the unhappiest of God's creatures.

If Beethoven was "living a wretched life" in 1801, it was not because his music was suffering. Quite the contrary. Year after year, Beethoven's writing had been gaining momentum and reaching new levels of maturity and excellence. "I live only in my notes," he wrote his friends, "and one composition is scarcely done before another is begun. As I am writing now, I often work on three or four pieces at once." Beethoven's confidence in his artistic powers was strengthening daily; only his deafness threatened to "put a spoke in his wheel," as he wrote to Franz Wegeler.

Around 1800, when he was thirty, Beethoven dared to venture outside the safe confines of the keyboard to venture into two worlds he eventually would master as had no other composer: the symphony and the string quartet. Beethoven's First Symphony contained many of the same features as his first piano sonatas. Firmly within the tradition of Mozart and Haydn, the work nonetheless had enough original touches to mark its creator as an audacious new talent. Almost as a joke, Beethoven had begun the piece in the wrong key, sending critical eyebrows sykward, and imbued the entire composition with a force and energy Vienna had not heard before. His first set of string quartets (six in all) were similarly received, as was his first published piano concerto.

However, it was still in his writing for solo piano that Beethoven experimented with and polished most completely his developing musical logic and style. In his piano sonatas he tackled and solved musical problems long before he faced them in other mediums. It was with the piano that Beethoven started to forge much of the new musical language that would remain his trademark for decades.

Progress was an essential artistic ideal for Beethoven. Living as he did in a time of immense change, he was determined to bring the process of development into his music. Each new composition was to be an advance on its predecessor; each new work was to penetrate further into the mysteries of musical art. Never content to rest on his musical laurels, Beethoven was always searching out purer and more immediate forms of musical communication.

The sonatas Beethoven wrote in the years just before and just after the turn of the century include some of his most famous, such as the *Moonlight* and *Pathétique*. The measured world of op. 2, no. 1 had within five short years given way to dramatic, emotionally compelling compositions that sounded a note of passion in music never before encountered. Simple rhythmic and melodic figures repeated again and again for maximum effect (as in the first movement of the *Moonlight* Sonata), massive chords and a spare but telling use of harmony increased Beethoven's expressive range. And Beethoven exploited the inherent drama of the sonata as never before. Development sections lengthened and took on increasing musical significance. The symmetry of the early sonatas began to give way to an organization that placed more and more emphasis on the finale. The *Moonlight* Sonata, for example, was a radical departure from tradition that saw a slow movement begin the composition and a demonic sonata movement end it.

Beethoven's musical experiments paid off. He began to be known as a revolutionary new composer, the center of a dedicated and enthusiastic following. He felt a new power bubbling up within him, a power in which he delighted. In the very same letters to Amenda and Wegeler in which he lamented his deafness, he described this force, as in this letter from the fall of 1801:

> If it were not for my deafness, I should before now have traveled over half the world, and that I must do. — There is no greater delight for me than to practice and show my art — Oh, if I were rid of this affliction I would embrace the world. Really, I feel that my youth is just beginning, for have I not always been in poor health? My physical strength has for some time past been steadily gaining and also my mental powers. Each day I move toward the goal which I sense but cannot describe, only in this way can your B. live.

Only his deafness stood between Beethoven and his unnameable goal. As long as he let himself believe that his hearing might improve or even be restored to normal, he could temporarily forget its shadow and enjoy his growing sense of artistic power. However, as the months and years passed, it became increasingly obvious that his affliction was permanent and unyielding. His deafness and his art were on a collision course. Eventually, Beethoven was going to have to confront the full extent of his tragedy. That confrontation came in the summer of 1802 in the little town of Heiligenstadt, outside Vienna.

Beethoven had been retiring to the country every summer since he had moved to Vienna, to compose and renew his love of nature. He did most of his writing for the year during these vacations, and the summer of 1802 proved especially productive. Between April and October, he wrote three violin sonatas (opus 30), three piano sonatas (opus 31), his Second Symphony and two important sets of piano variations. All these works share an assuredness Beethoven had not shown before. The symphony, in particular, is a joyous and energetic work.

But Beethoven's grief nonetheless intensified. The stay in

Heiligenstadt had been prolonged on the advice of his doctor, who felt that quiet and seclusion might bring some improvement in the composer's condition. Perhaps Beethoven himself felt that this was his last chance for a cure. But, if anything, things got worse. Ferdinand Ries, a friend and student of Beethoven's, visited him that summer in the country, and the two of them often took walks together. Recounts Ries:

> On one of these outings Beethoven gave me the first startling proof of his loss of hearing, which Stephan von Breuning had already mentioned to me. I called his attention to a shepherd in the forest who was piping very agreeably in the woods on a flute made of a twig of elder. For half an hour Beethoven could hear nothing, and though I assured him it was the same with me (which was not the case), he became extremely quiet and morose. When occasionally he seemed to be merry, it was generally to the extreme of boisterousness; but this happened seldom.

The solitude of Heiligenstadt, especially when broken by painful incidents like this one, brought Beethoven's inner turmoil to a head. He sat down in early fall and wrote an amazing letter, addressed but never sent to his two brothers, Carl and Johann (although Johann's name is mysteriously left blank throughout the document). The letter was not found until after Beethoven's death, twenty-five years later. In it Beethoven summed up all the torments his deafness had caused him. As a confessional document, it has only one rival in Beethoven's life, a love letter he was to write a decade later. The Heiligenstadt Testament, as this is called, is worth quoting in its entirety. No more poignant document exists in the history of music.

For my brothers Carl and ——— *Beethoven*
Oh you men who think or say that I am malevolent, stubborn

or misanthropic, how greatly do you wrong me. You do not know the secret cause which makes me seem that way to you. From childhood on my heart and soul have been full of the tender feeling of goodwill, and I was ever inclined to accomplish great things. But, think that for 6 years now I have been hopelessly afflicted, made worse by senseless physicians, from year to year deceived with hopes of improvement, finally compelled to face the prospect of a lasting malady (whose cure will take years or, perhaps, be impossible). Though born with a fiery, active temperament, even susceptible to the diversions of society, I was soon compelled to withdraw myself, to live life alone. If at times I tried to forget all this, oh how harshly was I flung back by the doubly sad experience of my bad hearing. Yet it was impossible for me to say to people, "Speak louder, shout, for I am deaf." Ah, how could I possibly admit an infirmity in the one sense which ought to be more perfect in me than in others, a sense which I once possessed in the highest perfection, a perfection such as few in my profession enjoy or ever have enjoyed. — Oh, I cannot do it, therefore forgive me when you see me draw back when I would have gladly mingled with you. My misfortune is doubly painful to me because I am bound to be misunderstood; for me there can be no relation with my fellow men, no refined conversations, no mutual exchange of ideas. I must live almost alone like one who has been banished, I can mix with society only as much as true necessity demands. If I approach near to people a hot terror seizes upon me and I fear being exposed to the danger that my condition might be noticed. Thus it has been during the last six months which I have spent in the country. By ordering me to spare my hearing as much as possible, my intelligent doctor almost fell in with my own present frame of mind, though sometimes I ran counter to it by yielding to my desire for companionship. But what a humiliation for me when someone standing next to me heard a flute in the distance and I heard nothing, or someone heard a shepherd singing and again I heard nothing. Such incidents drove me almost to despair, a little more of that and I would have ended my life — it was only my art that held me back. Ah, it seemed impossible to leave the world until I had brought forth all that I felt was within me. So I endured this wretched existence — truly wretched for so susceptible a body which can be thrown by a sudden change from the best condition to the very worst. — Patience, they say, is what I must choose for my guide, and I have done so — I hope my determination will remain firm to endure until it pleases the inexorable Parcae to break the thread. Perhaps I shall get better, perhaps not, I am ready — Forced to become a philosopher already in my 28th year, oh it is not easy, and for the artist much more difficult than for anyone else. — Divine One, thou seest my inmost soul, thou knowest that therein dwells the love of mankind and the desire to do good. — Oh fellow men, when at some point you read this, consider then that you have done me an injustice; someone who has misfortune may console himself to find a similar case to his, who despite all the limitations of Nature nevertheless did everything within his powers to become accepted among worthy artists and men. You my brothers Carl and ——— as soon as I am dead if Dr. Schmidt is still alive ask him in my name to describe my malady, and attach this written document to his account of my illness so that as far as is possible at least the world may become reconciled to me after my death. — At the same time I declare you two to be the heirs to my small fortune (if so it can be called); divide it fairly; bear with and help each other. What injury you have done me you know was long ago forgiven. To you, brother Carl, I give special thanks for the attachment you have shown me of late. It is my wish that you may have a better and freer life than I have had.

the temple of nature and mankind— Never? — No — Oh that would be too hard.

The Heiligenstadt Testament — part confession, part lament, part will — remains the single most compelling document Beethoven ever wrote. We see in the despair, the anger, the digressions and especially in the final postscript a portrait of a soul in torment, and a will frustrated by fate, unsure of how it will continue. What we cannot see in the testament is that it represents the end of a process of grief for Beethoven, not the beginning. Either through the crisis it speaks of or through the writing of the document itself, Beethoven seems to have purged himself of the fears and doubts he roughly but eloquently describes. Only once again in the next ten years did Beethoven refer in writing to his deafness; it is as though having written his will he had come to terms with the prime difficulty of his life.

Deafness had seemed to be the one obstacle that might prevent Beethoven from accomplishing all he wished as an artist. Somehow in Heiligenstadt he realized that he had the power to remove that threat simply by willing himself to do so. He was not going to hear again, but he would not stop living or working on that account. He had decided to continue. That decision was the most significant one he ever made.

The testament marks the boundary point between two eras in Beethoven's life and work. On the one side is his youth, his apprenticeship, his growing artistic maturity and confidence. On the other side is the heroic artist that he was to become over the next ten years. Beethoven, as we shall see, was forced to give up a great deal to achieve what he felt was his destiny, and the Heiligenstadt Testament documents that loss. However, he had gained something as well. When Beethoven left the little town in the fall of 1802, the seeds had already been planted for the composition that would announce his new artistic presence to the world.

9

Breakthrough: The *Eroica*

eethoven returned to Vienna after the Heiligenstadt summer and fall infused with a new vigor. He bubbled over with enthusiasm in letters to his publishers about the works he had composed in the country. No one could have suspected the torments that had accompanied those compositions. At thirty-two, Beethoven was finally ready to pour all of his creative energy into one massive work — his Third Symphony, the *Eroica* (the Heroic).

Beethoven had been a successful, even a daring, composer before the *Eroica*. But nothing in his previous portfolio could have prepared his audiences for this gargantuan symphony, which sounded a passionate note never before encountered in Western music. The *Eroica* was Beethoven's bold throwing down of the gauntlet to his peers, a herald of a new artistic sensibility and a new conception of music. It is one of those landmarks in the history of art that mark the end of one era and the beginning of another.

The Beethoven we know today was born with the *Eroica*. In it he first sounded that note of personal heroism and defiance of fate we now associate with all of his music. He seems to have created a new language overnight, filling the work with novel techniques and ideas he had never used before. His Second Symphony, written only a year earlier in Heiligenstadt, is still a "modern" version of the symphonic forms Mozart and Haydn had invented in the 1770s and 1780s. The *Eroica* is a new work, with new proportions, aesthetics and artistic aims. From start to finish it is conceived on a monumental scale, its four massive movements taking almost an hour to perform. The Second Symphony is no more than half its size.

However, it was not just the *Eroica's* emotional power and musical innovation that made it noteworthy in 1803 and 1804. The *Eroica* rendered in sound the ideals of the French Revolution, the great movement that had liberated Europe — or so it was thought — from centuries of superstition and inequity, the force that still inspires much political passion today. The *Eroica* allows us to relive the joy and excitement of those early days of the Revolution, days when, according to William Wordsworth, "Bliss it was to be alive / But to be young was very heaven."

The extra-musical associations of the *Eroica* were somewhat hidden from its first audiences, who accepted the work simply as Beethoven's Third Symphony. When it was published, the subtitle "Heroic" was added to describe the work's emotional power. However, the *Eroica* has a much more explicit message. Throughout its gestation and well into its composition, the symphony was entitled "Bonaparte," and was intended as a musical portrait of Napoleon. Ferdinand Ries, Beethoven's friend and student, confirmed the connection in his memoirs:

> In this symphony Beethoven had Buonaparte in mind, but as he was when he was First Consul. Beethoven esteemed him greatly at the time and likened him to the greatest Roman consuls. I as well as several of his more intimate friends saw a copy of the score lying upon his table, with the word "Buonaparte" at the extreme top of the title page, and at the extreme bottom "Luigi van Beethoven," but not another word. Whether, and

with what the space between was to be filled out, I do not know.

All Europe had followed the career of Napoleon Bonaparte since he had risen from obscurity to become the leader of revolutionary France. Originally an officer in the French army during Robespierre's Reign of Terror, Napoleon had in 1799 staged a coup d'état to save the Revolution. As first consul he had transformed France and spread its revolutionary promise of "liberté, egalité et fraternité" across Europe. Europe was fascinated by Bonaparte, especially its intelligentsia. The "world-soul on horseback," as Hegel called him, seemed to embody all the ideals of a half-century of Enlightenment thought and political struggle. Napoleon seemed the archetypal hero, a brilliant military strategist whose personal courage and vision spread the healing balm of liberty across a continent suffering the torment of social enslavement. How could nations tasting for the first time the sweetness of liberty and the prospect of a better life ahead not fall under his spell? To many, Beethoven among them, Bonaparte represented the spirit of a new age of progress. Some celebrated the achievements of the great liberator in words; Beethoven represented the hopes of Europe in sound.

Beethoven had followed Napoleon and the progress of the Revolution with more than passing interest. He had enthusiastically espoused the ideals of the Enlightenment in Bonn, where their intellectual allure had been happily connected for him with the charm of the von Breuning family. His deafness and the challenge it presented him only intensified his belief in the significance of the inner man, as well as the need to confront and defeat all adversaries. Napoleon seemed to represent all these values; he was a hero to Beethoven as he was to so many other Europeans of his generation.

But Beethoven and Europe were to be bitterly disappointed by their new god. In May of 1804, Napoleon had himself crowned emperor of France. This champion of liberty had taken on the most repugnant of all tyrannical garments, the imperial mantle. The promise of egalitarianism that Napoleon had once represented had been cruelly mocked. In Vienna, Ferdinand Ries was one of the first to hear the news. He ran to Beethoven, who was just preparing the final manuscript of the *Eroica*. In Ries's words:

> I was the first to bring him the intelligence that Buonaparte had declared himself Emperor, whereupon he flew into a rage and cried out: "Is he then, too, nothing more than an ordinary human being? Now he, too, will trample on the rights of man and indulge only his ambition. He will exalt himself above all others, become a tyrant!" Beethoven went to the table, took hold of the title page by the top, tore it in two and threw it on the floor. The first page was rewritten and only then did the symphony receive the title: "Sinfonia eroica."

Another musician witnessed Beethoven's outburst, so Ries's story is unquestionably true. Yet Beethoven did not give up the reference to Bonaparte quite as quickly as Ries imagined. A copy of the *Eroica* still preserved and dated August 1804 carries the title "Grand Symphony composed on Bonaparte." Only when the work was published in 1806 did all mention of Napoleon disappear from the title page of Beethoven's Third Symphony.

Still more slowly did Napoleon retreat from Beethoven's heart. As late as 1809, with French troops occupying Vienna and Beethoven in a consequent fury, an acquaintance could write of the composer:

> His mind was much occupied with the greatness of Napoleon, and he often spoke to me about it. Through all his resentment I could see that he admired his rise from such obscure beginnings; his democratic ideas were flattered by it.

Beethoven more than admired Napoleon, he identified quite powerfully with the Corsican general. The similarities between the two are striking. They were virtually the same age. Both rose from modest personal circumstances to achieve greatness in their chosen fields; both were inflamed early with the ideals of the Enlightenment, which they sought to make real in the world. Both remained outsiders even after their triumphs, Napoleon because of an odd coldness of personality, Beethoven because of his deafness. It is not hard to imagine that as Beethoven felt his artistic power growing within him in the early years of the nineteenth century, he would see in Napoleon another soul driven by a similar mission, similarly heroic, similarly alone. Beethoven even fancied testing himself against Napoleon. More than once he imagined meeting him on the battlefield. "It is a pity I do not understand the art of war as well as I do the art of music," he once told a friend. "I would defeat him."

Despite Beethoven's subsequent disillusion, the *Eroica* is perhaps still best symbolized by the title page Ries first saw for it: two names on a single page, Bonaparte and Beethoven, with nothing in between — a double portrait of heroism and achievement.

The *Eroica* is such a massive work that analyses of it have filled thousands of pages. Each of the work's four movements is written on a scale new to Beethoven, although each has its antecedents in Beethoven's previous compositions. Although the first movement is a gargantuan seven hundred bars in length (the first movement of op. 2, no. 1 is 152 bars long), it is still clearly written in sonata form. The second, slow movement is actually a funeral march, unheard of in a symphony but a style Beethoven had used in a previous piano sonata. This movement, too, is written in sonata form. The third movement, a scherzo, is Beethoven's transformation of the stately minuet and trio that had graced symphonies for close to seventy years. Written to the same formal structure as a minuet and trio, the third movement of the *Eroica* is a turbulent portrait of a great soul at play, the kind of play one might encounter on Olympus. The final movement of the symphony is an enormous theme and variations, a reworking of the same theme and some of the same variations that Beethoven had used for his *Eroica* piano variations, written during the Heiligenstadt summer. Short of spelling it out on the score, Beethoven could not have made a clearer connection between the symphony and the torments of Heiligenstadt than this borrowing from himself.

Everything about the *Eroica* is big, and even today the scope and range of the symphony can catch an audience by surprise. In 1803, the piece was considered impossibly long and difficult, a work of willful eccentricity. Critical opinion of the symphony was deeply divided. There was a minority who immediately celebrated the originality of the work and a majority who found it incomprehensible. Most listeners just found it too long, like the man at its premiere who shouted from the balcony during the final movement: "I'll pay another kreutzer if the thing will just stop!" It didn't.

With all the work's novelties, it is its opening movement that is the most original and that shows Beethoven's new-found confidence at its freshest. When you listen to it, you will hear its power immediately and can imagine how miraculous its appearance must have seemed in 1804.

Although the first movement of the *Eroica* is longer and more complex than anything Beethoven had written before, it is still organized in sonata form, with its exposition, development and recapitulation. Beethoven used the clarity of that organization to help him expand his musical language and universe.

The *Eroica* announces its character right from the beginning. It starts with two massive chords for full orchestra in E-flat, the work's home key. The simplicity of these introductory cannon shots announces the key of the symphony as well as its emotional landscape: bold, decisive, powerful. It was common at that time to precede a symphony with a slow introduction, to help ease an audience into the experience. These two chords are Beethoven's idea of a slow introduction. With two fists pounding on the door, he plunges us immediately into the musical action.

As we've now come to expect, the main musical idea for this massive first movement is presented right at the opening.

What a plain and uninteresting bit of music this theme seems to be. It's really nothing more than the notes of an E-flat triad (chord) played in succession. It seems impossible that a movement of seven hundred bars could be based on such a bare idea. But it was just such basic musical material that Beethoven relished and used for all his middle-period masterpieces. The extreme simplicity of these primary ideas — their granite-like impermeability — allowed Beethoven to use them to build immense musical structures. As well, their austerity gave his work a sort of primal directness and honesty.

Thus, the main theme of the *Eroica*'s first movement may be simple, but there is something strong and vital about it as well, especially that ascent to the fifth that characterizes its second half. As a heroic motif, it will do just fine.

However, on its first appearance in the piece, Beethoven seems curiously ambivalent about his own idea. Listen to the opening a couple of times. Notice how that E-flat triad veers off into a harmonically ambiguous area just as it ends, while at the same time the pulse of the music gets lost (just for a few seconds, mind you) before all is righted and the music continues. It seems an odd way to begin a work, even though the moment is brief. Why did Beethoven do it?

The secret to the first movement of the *Eroica* and to much of the music Beethoven wrote after it is his ability to stretch sonata form, expanding its sections while maintaining their order and proportions.

Giving the music away too early is fatal to this approach. So Beethoven holds back the immediate resolution of his musical ideas, allowing them time to develop to their full emotional power. This somewhat irresolute opening of the *Eroica* is a perfect example of the technique. We will see that the "explanation" of this idea will come only hundreds of bars later.

Beethoven also used another technique to expand the *Eroica*'s scale and scope. Rather than present single themes once or twice and then move on to other, different ideas, Beethoven created larger thematic sections, still organized by a single idea but made up of more musical events. That's what happens at the beginning of the *Eroica*. That first theme acts as the focal point of several musical ideas, providing the glue that holds them together.

The entire package thus functions as the *a* section of the exposition. After Beethoven introduces his main idea the first time and creates that momentary digression, he returns to it immediately. The theme is repeated in the winds (flutes and clarinets), and then just the second half of the idea is thrown back and forth between the strings and winds, in exactly the same manner as Beethoven extended his first idea in op. 2, no. 1. This by-play leads to what sounds like a new musical thought, a descending figure that turns into a brief syncopated section for full orchestra. Syncopation is a device whereby a composer puts the rhythmical stress on the wrong beat — the accent on the wrong musical syl-LAB-le — to blur the pulse of the music as well as disturb the peace of the listener, who momentarily loses the downbeat of the music. Beethoven loved the emotional effect of syncopation and used it frequently. You can hear the syncopation in the harshly accented chords that accompany this new musical idea. We might think we're in a new section of the piece with this idea, but Beethoven makes it clear that we are still in the *a* section of the exposition by replaying his main theme immediately. Ever sensitive to his audience, Beethoven constantly balances the familiar with the unfamiliar.

Now, however, we are ready to move toward the second theme of the *Eroica*'s exposition. That final statement of the main theme dissolves into a thinner texture, and a transition theme appears — a simple, three-note descending idea — which is repeated several times in the woodwinds while the lower strings march up and down a major triad. The idea ends abruptly as the full orchestra takes it up, and a second, sweeter idea takes its place, but just for a second. This second idea is itself superseded by a third, a quick descending figure in the strings, which sounds a bit like a Bach fugue. Just as in the exposition, Beethoven doesn't just give us one transition theme, but several. But don't let his expanded time scales throw you off. Despite all this musical activity, we're still in the transition section between themes *a* and *b* in the exposition. We may take longer to get from one place to another than we did in op. 2, no. 1, but we're still using the same map.

The third transition theme inaugurates a much longer section, which builds to a quite definite climax and conclusion, making us feel that we finally have moved from one section in the music to another. If you listen carefully, you might also realize that we have moved from one key to another as well — a sure sign that we are about to begin the exposition's *b* section.

We would normally expect a hot new theme from Beethoven at this point, as a contrast to the first, but what we get instead is somewhat disappointing (for a reason we won't understand for several hundred bars). The "theme" is virtually a single note repeated over two bars by the woodwind family — hardly a melody at all. And Beethoven scarcely develops this idea; he repeats it just once before reducing his orchestra to a hushed piano. Then, out of the ashes of this first *b* theme, comes another. Plucked (pizzicato) strings emerge softly, building in volume to introduce a new idea — a descending major triad with a heavy accent on the fourth note. Beethoven is adding several ideas together as he did in both the *a* and transition sections of the exposition, to help him expand the time scale of sonata form.

This second *b* theme leads to another thrilling syncopated section for full orchestra, in which the pulse of the music is entirely lost for several bars. This is an eerie and terrible moment, one that must have shocked the Viennese audiences at its premiere. A raw power in the music has broken through the artificial order of the bar lines. Emotion has swept away the old conventions, as a conqueror pushes aside the vanquished. The hero speaks in these bars — Napoleon and Beethoven both.

This mighty passage of orchestral chords is finally interrupted by a simple ascending triad in the cellos and basses — a reminder of the first theme of the movement — before the momentum builds again to form a coda to the exposition, again based on a syncopated figure. The main theme is clearly heard at the exposition's close in a series of horribly dissonant chords.

Beethoven had never written a more forceful exposition; it breathes power and consciousness of power. Nonetheless there is a certain terseness about it. The profusion of fragmented ideas — none fully developed — gives the impression of something being held back, something yet to come. Listen for this fragmentation in the repeat of the exposition, but notice as well that this cornucopia of ideas is still organized in sonata form, with a first theme, transition section, second theme and coda. What is new is that each section is made up of more than one musical idea. Once you get used to this approach, the form of the music falls easily into place.

We mentioned earlier that as Beethoven matured as a composer, the development sections of his sonatas increased in both size and importance. The development of the *Eroica* was the first of these massive sections. Beethoven had written some fairly lengthy and demanding development sections before this symphony, but nothing to compare with what we find here. For the first time, the true otherness — the "away-ness" — of the development section is fully exploited. We see now one of the reasons Beethoven was holding back in the exposition; it was in the development that he wished to concentrate his musical intensity.

Both as a way of calming his audiences after the rough power of the exposition's coda and as a means of expanding his formal plan, Beethoven begins the development with a slow, atmospheric section, like taking a big breath before an important dive into the unknown. Then he begins.

We have come to expect the unexpected from Beethoven's developments, but he still can catch us by surprise, as he does here. Rather than using his main theme or any of the other thematic ideas he introduced in the exposition, Beethoven begins the development with the little three-note figure he tossed our way in the first transition section. It is an idea we have surely forgotten by now, since it went by so quickly in the exposition and was given so little prominence. Here it is given a new significance. Beethoven loved to use dramatic surprise in this way, by finding new meaning in seemingly minor musical details. It is exactly the way a mystery writer sprinkles clues through a plot, so that an offhand remark in chapter 3 can become the key to the entire mystery a hundred pages later.

This little transition figure cycles through three repeats, harmonies changing each time, before Beethoven lands in C minor to begin the first episode in the development's plot. It is an episode that stars the *Eroica*'s main idea, the one that began the work. Beethoven didn't use much of that idea in the exposition, so he has plenty of opportunity to play around with it now, twisting and turning it to develop new musical possibilities.

Repeated for almost thirty bars, that opening idea now holds sway over the music. Deep in the lower register of the orchestra, the main motif rocks back and forth, changing harmonies with each repetition, building in scope and power. After two repetitions, Beethoven adds another twist. While the main idea is heard in the lower strings, the upper strings play that Bach-like figure that first appeared in the transition section in the exposition. Nothing was wasted in Beethoven's mature style. Few ideas are just tossed out and left alone. Fragments of music that seem to have nothing to do with one another are combined to form new, perfect combinations.

The main theme and this transition theme are heard once, there's a pause for a breath, and then they are heard again. Beethoven's instincts told him that the excessive fragmentation of the exposition needed to be balanced by a more stable section in the development in order to continue to expand the time scale of the movement.

The development's next episode once again begins with that three-note figure that had inaugurated the development a few bars earlier. Another surprise. We had hardly expected to hear that little theme once in the development, let alone twice. And Beethoven continues the surprise by making that theme itself the center of the next episode. It is turned into a mini-fugue and tossed about the various sections of the orchestra for twenty bars or so. For a second, the music takes on a lighter, airy character.

But not for long. Out of this sunny parody of the eighteenth century, Beethoven plunges us into the darkness of the twentieth. In a series of almost forty full orchestral chords off the beat that continues for nearly two pages in the score, the metrical pulse of the music is completely lost in a musical cosmos of no fixed boundaries, a primeval sonic world. Dissonances pile up on one another, harmonies collide, and the music mounts to an almost unbearable intensity. It is a volcanic eruption of sound, carrying everything before it in a stream of energy.

It was moments like this one that so completely defined Beethoven's new musical aesthetic. Music of such intensity was unimaginable to a generation that had been raised on a civilized diet of Mozart and Haydn. Here was the Revolution expressed in tones, a new world of feeling that excited as many as it mystified. Here was a new voice.

After this outburst we are completely in Beethoven's hands, with no idea of what is to follow. What could possibly follow an earth-quake? A composer cannot write such a disordering moment of music and then return to a familiar idea. Something new must appear.

And it does, an idea that Beethoven has been holding in reserve for 150 bars, half the movement. Here, in the middle of the develop-ment, Beethoven provides us with his true second theme, the one that never really appeared in the exposition. You can almost hear the theme being born in the heavy chords that precede it. Forget the fact that the theme is in the "wrong" key (E minor) or in the "wrong" place in the form. Beethoven's impeccable sense of musical logic told him that the stretched dimensions of his movement made the place-ment of the second theme here a necessity. We needed to wait this long for the contrasting strength of this theme to work to maximum advantage. Earlier, it would have been swallowed up by the power of the movement's main idea and extinguished by the storms of the development. Here, it provides exactly the change of texture the movement needs.

This new theme in the development is everything the package of fragmented second themes in the exposition was not. Lovely and lyri-cal, with its minor key and singing style, it provides a true contrast to the main triadic idea with which the movement began. And if there are any doubts about how seriously we are to take this new theme, Beethoven removes them right away. The whole idea is repeated twice, with no skittering interruptions like those in the exposition. This is a musical idea Beethoven wants us to register.

As well, to reinforce the contrast essential to sonata form, Beethoven suddenly moves to a major key and gives us the main tri-adic theme once more. Never before had the main idea of a piece appeared with such surprising effect in a development. With a new theme just introduced, the last thing we expect at this point is to be wrenched back to the beginning of the movement. But we are for a few bars, as the main theme turns from a major to a minor color, and then, just as abruptly, the new minor theme reappears and is further developed. In effect, what Beethoven has done here is re-create in the development the relationship of first and second theme that normally appears in the exposition. Beethoven may have pushed sonata form in many new directions in this movement, but, as we have noted before, he never questioned its basic musical principles. His genius consisted in creating a perfect mixture of striking originality and traditional form.

Having established the relationship between these two thematic ideas, Beethoven provides what can only be described as a coda to the development, a closing section that will take us back to our starting point.

As the new "second theme" comes to a gentle close, the music becomes hushed, then begins to build once again. The winds play the main theme over and over in a spiral of growing intensity. In contrast, the lower strings begin a series of ascending pizzicato steps that get louder with each repetition. These sounded to Sir George Grove, a leading nineteenth-century Beethoven scholar, like someone "stalking over the world as none but a hero can stalk, and making us feel like pygmies as we listen to his determined and elastic footfalls."

The music rises toward its inevitable climax — but it is a climax that never comes. Instead, the music slows down, quietens and takes on an air of mystery. After two hundred bars of sound and fury, the development of the *Eroica* expires in a fog of anticipation and suspense. The texture is spare, the music soft. And then out of the fog, while the strings are still holding their spooky tremolo, a lone horn sounds a familiar refrain. It is the beginning of the main motif, now announced like a hunting call in the mist of a spring dawn.

A lot has been written about this little call, because it is the biggest "mistake" Beethoven wrote into the *Eroica*: it seems as though the horn player has gotten ahead of the rest of the orchestra and begun the recapitulation two bars early. At least that's what

Ferdinand Ries thought at the first rehearsal of the *Eroica* (a disaster by all accounts). Standing next to Beethoven, Ries exploded when he heard the horn come in as written: "That damned horn player!" he cried. "Can't he count? It sounds terrible!" Ries looked over to Beethoven and immediately realized his mistake. He adds, "I believe I was very close indeed to having my ears boxed at that moment — Beethoven was a long time in forgiving me."

As was musical Europe a long time in forgiving Beethoven. For many years, this supposed faux pas was "corrected" in performances of the *Eroica*, even by great conductors, who forced the horn to come in with everyone else two bars later. But this entry is no mistake. It is Beethoven's way of breaking expectations and providing his recapitulation with the drama it would otherwise lack. It is a perfect close to a development that has broken all the traditional rules of sonata composition.

However, this powerful development section — longer by itself than many complete sonata movements and exploiting for the first time the dramatic possibilities of the form — poses a problem for Beethoven. He has to be careful not to let the recapitulation destroy the momentum so carefully built up so far in this movement with a simple-minded repetition of the exposition. We must hear some version of the exposition now; the whole basis of the form — its home-away-home pattern — depends on it. But a too conventional end to the movement will rob it of its individuality, originality and power.

Beethoven gives us a hint of how he is going to solve this problem right at the beginning of the recap. Remember how he veered away from his first statement of the main theme at the beginning of the movement, just after it was announced. Listen to what happens in the recap at exactly the same point: the music changes to a new key and to a new section not heard in the exposition. And not just any new section. The horn — the musical embodiment of the movement's "hero" — sings out the main theme, but with a new top note. The theme goes triumphantly up at the end rather than down, and this top note is held for five bars. The flute then repeats the new pattern. The moment is short but important. Beethoven is hinting to us that the "real" main theme — the true musical basis for the movement — was not the version we heard at the beginning of the piece; that version was just a sampling of what was to come. The real theme, the real point of the music, is to be found here in the movement's conclusion.

Once these bars pass, Beethoven does launch into a fairly conventional recapitulation. We return to E-flat major, and, with a couple of variations to make sure the second theme group is heard in the home key, the recap continues very much like the exposition. Here are the same transition ideas, second-theme package, syncopations leading to a coda and conclusion on a group of dissonant chords.

Many if not most movements written in sonata form would end here, with the restoration of the exposition and the main key complete. However, were the *Eroica*'s first movement to do so, the effect would be profoundly disappointing. On one of your listens, imagine the movement ending with this conclusion of the recapitulation. It would be an emotional and musical disaster. We have gone through too much upheaval in the development to feel satisfied with a conventional recapitulation. To return to the measured proportions of the exposition after the wild power of the development would seem cynical, incomplete. In expanding the proportions of his development, Beethoven broke the normal mold of sonata form. Now he has to do something to fix it.

And he does. It was not uncommon to finish off sonata movements with a small concluding coda, a little jewel tacked onto the end of the movement to provide a greater sense of finality. (Op. 2, no. 1 had such a coda, if you remember.) In the *Eroica*, this little jewel becomes the Hope Diamond, a massive section of almost 150 bars that not only provides a proper counterbalance to the equally massive development, but also becomes the movement's climax. After a series of false approaches, here, at the very end of the movement, Beethoven can finally let go. He has saved to the very end the apotheosis of his work. The recapitulation, with its predictable repetition, will not end the movement. A new powerful coda will do so instead.

So those dissonant chords that end the recapitulation do not end the movement. Instead Beethoven has the orchestra repeat the main theme a few times in different keys, as though they were trying to find one they liked. Notice how neutral this section sounds. Beethoven's audiences would have had no idea of where they were going at this point. The feeling of suspense could not be stronger.

Beethoven toys with this suspense as long as he can. He plays his main theme in three separate keys; each time the music goes nowhere. Finally, quietly, the lower strings begin repeating the main theme with the violins adding a lovely counterpoint on top. This is a bit of music we have not heard before; Beethoven is treating his coda like a second development. The mood here is gentle and idyllic compared with the storms that ended the recapitulation.

The gentle violin line leads effortlessly to what is both a surprise and not a surprise at the same time: a reprise of the "true" second theme, the one Beethoven introduced in the development. We need to hear this theme again for the movement to make musical sense; too much was made of it in the development for it to just disappear. However, since a theme introduced for the first time in the development could never reappear in a regular recapitulation, Beethoven was forced to use the coda to remain faithful to the principle of sonata form that demanded a final accounting of all the movement's musical characters.

Now Beethoven is ready to finally end the movement and reveal its musical secrets. The striding hero idea we heard at the end of the development returns, but this time it does not fritter away into the mysterious atmosphere that ended the development. Now it leads inexorably to the final musical statement of this enormous first movement.

Out of that striding motif in the strings comes a solo horn with a version of the main motif we have not heard before, a two-part idea that goes up to a triumphant fifth at the end of the motif and then repeats itself, ending on that fifth again. This expanded version of the theme makes us feel we are hearing the complete musical idea for the first time. Up to now, we have just been fed fragments of it. Interestingly, it is in this form — the one heard for the first time more than six hundred bars into this movement — that the idea first appeared in Beethoven's sketchbooks. This is the true first theme of the piece, hinted at throughout but revealed only at the end.

Having journeyed through exposition, development, recapitulation and coda to reach his goal, Beethoven basks in the musical light of his success. After its first statement on the horn, this climactic idea is played in both upper and lower strings, as an accompaniment motif trips along with it like children running alongside the carriage of a triumphal march. The power of the music builds, until the motif bursts out of the assembled brass. At its very end, the movement has reached its climax.

A transition passage borrowed from the exposition leads the music out of this final apotheosis to a short coda and three powerful chords, the exact counterparts to the two chords that began the movement. The first movement ends as it began, with announcements of power.

I can confidently assert that no matter how many times you listen to the opening movement of the *Eroica*, or to its other three movements, you will always hear something you had missed before. The music is so rich and exciting, it never wears out. No wonder its first audiences were mystified by this explosion of sound. They would have been stunned as much by the work's novelty as by its combination of raw energy, triumphant force, technical innovation and sheer exuberance. The *Eroica* not only provided endless opportunities for musicians to explore its secrets, it changed the way Europe conceived of music altogether.

Beethoven's combination of the monumental and the intimate in the *Eroica*, with music that spanned empires yet spoke with an individual voice, set the standard for the next decade of his career. The breakthrough he had sensed in the early years of the nineteenth century, but could not describe, had taken place. Fears of his deafness now conquered, Beethoven embarked on a period of composition that was to see one masterpiece after another tumble from his pen. He was about to begin what has been called his heroic decade.

Most of the music Beethoven wrote during these ten years was instrumental, communicating in the special language of pure sound. But one of the first of these masterworks was his only opera, *Fidelio*. *Fidelio* is as close a companion piece to the *Eroica* as Beethoven ever composed. Both shine with the light of the Revolution and the ideals for which it originally stood. Both reveal essential features of Beethoven's heart and soul. But *Fidelio* adds one extra dimension to the *Eroica*. It celebrates Beethoven's conception of the ideal woman, and introduces into his art an echo of the conflicted and confused relationships with women that were to play a greater role in his life as he left its morning and entered its afternoon and evening.

10

Fidelio:
The Hymn to Liberty

*L*éonore, ou L'Amour conjugale (Leonora, or Married Love) was written in 1799 by the French playwright J. N. Bouilly, just as Napoleon was asserting his power over France as first consul. A story of love, revenge and oppression, *Léonore* could have emerged only from a country ravaged by a decade of civil war. Although something of a melodramatic potboiler, *Léonore* had the power to inspire two other operas before Beethoven began his setting in the waning months of 1804. Though it cost him much grief and enormous effort, Beethoven's *Léonore* (renamed *Fidelio* a week before its premiere) has become one of the greatest tributes to liberty and the emancipation of the human spirit ever created.

Beethoven was not a natural man of the musical theater. Unlike his great predecessor Mozart, Beethoven lacked the chameleon-like ability to adapt to any musical character and portray any musical emotion. Mozart was the great observer, dispassionately recording the foibles and follies of his operatic characters and impeccably rendering their personalities into sound. Beethoven operated on a different artistic plane. He belonged to a generation of artists who believed that their own souls were mirrors of a universal soul. To reflect themselves was thus to reflect the world. Rather than look outside themselves for their inspiration, they looked within.

However, when Beethoven finally found a libretto (opera script) whose story inspired him, the resulting combination of personal emotion and objective drama could be powerful. Bouilly's *Léonore* was just such a libretto. Its story centers on a woman whose husband has been falsely imprisoned by his political enemy. Disguised as a man, Léonore desperately tries to find and rescue him. Risking her own life, she liberates her husband, as well as all of his fellow prisoners, and causes the downfall of the wicked jailer.

This "rescue" story, common in the literature inspired by the French Revolution and the Reign of Terror, nonetheless triggered some of Beethoven's most deeply felt convictions, emotions that even the recently composed *Eroica* had not sufficiently explored. If the *Eroica* was about heroism, *Fidelio* was about freedom, sacrifice and the eternal love of a woman for a man. Although he wrote only the music to the opera, its text and story still stand as Beethoven's personal manifesto.

Fidelio was a never-ending series of calamities for the composer and his collaborators. Beethoven was dissatisfied with the original libretto and demanded significant changes to it virtually up to opening night. Eventually, large parts of it were scrapped. The Austrian censor had his eye on the opera, on the lookout for revolutionary sentiments that might prove politically embarrassing. For reasons never clearly explained, the censor demanded the name change from *Léonore* to *Fidelio* a week before the premiere, completely confusing Beethoven's audiences. Worse, only two weeks before the opera was to open, French troops muscled their way into Vienna, occupied the city and sent its aristocrats scurrying to their country estates. Too late to change its premiere, *Fidelio* opened in November of 1805 to a half-empty house of French occupying officers. It was a disaster.

But the makeup of the opening night audience was not *Fidelio*'s only problem; it was also too long and dramatically inept. Too many characters and situations dissipated the energy of the drama and robbed the music of its cumulative power. Soon after its fall premiere, Beethoven's associates prevailed upon him to make significant changes to the shape of the work for a spring revival. Beethoven agreed, but the 1806 revival was no more successful than the original. Only during the heady days of the Congress of Vienna, eight years later, was *Fidelio* again revised and remounted. This time it was a roaring success. The *Fidelio* we listen to today is that 1814 version.

Two major bouts of reconstructive surgery have left their scars on the opera. Characters introduced at one point all but disappear from view, victims of one or another of the revisions. Sometimes the action is very drawn out, then jumps much too quickly from one scene to the next. Lengthy scene changes have audiences sitting in the dark at key dramatic moments. However, these problems were not serious enough to dim the integrity and emotion of Beethoven's score 180 years ago, nor are they today. The music of *Fidelio* washes all its dramatic faults clean.

Listening to opera is at once simpler and more difficult than listening to purely instrumental music. Simpler because there is a story that gives the music its form; you don't have to worry about expositions and recapitulations in an opera but need only follow the plot. More difficult because these plots are sometimes fantastic, unbelievable and confusing, especially if the opera is sung in a language foreign to you. However, don't make the mistake of ignoring the storyline when you listen to opera. Many of the musical effects in the score are tied to the words, so to miss the connection is to miss much of the composer's skill. A recording with a translated libretto is the ideal means for learning to enjoy opera. With repeated listenings, you can blend the interwoven dramatic and musical structures that make opera such a satisfying artform.

Fidelio's plot is no exception to the operatic rule. The opera is set in seventeenth-century Spain, although its eighteenth-century French author clearly meant his work to carry a contemporary message. Don Pizarro, governor of the Seville prison, has secretly incarcerated his enemy, Florestan, deep within its dungeons. To conceal his deed, he has told Florestan's former associate, the royal minister Don Fernando, that his friend is dead. When Pizarro gets word that Fernando is about to visit the prison, he conceives a desperate plan. To hide his deception, he will murder Florestan and bury him in the prison. He will enlist the aid of the old jailer Rocco in his crime.

Meanwhile, Florestan's wife, Leonora, has come to work for Rocco to try to find her husband. Disguised as a man named Fidelio, Leonora has not only won the heart of Rocco's daughter, Marsellina, but has also gained enough of the jailer's confidence to be permitted to accompany him into the prison and view the mysterious inmate he hardly dares speak of. Leonora will be Rocco's unwitting accomplice.

For an opera with such a dramatic story, *Fidelio* begins in a surprisingly light-hearted vein. After a fairly restrained overture, the action opens with Marsellina bantering with Jacquino, the jail's gatekeeper. He is pressing her to declare her love for him, an affection that might have blossomed had not the newcomer, Fidelio, entered the picture. The music is bright and Mozartian, giving little hint of what is to come. The Marsellina-Jacquino-Fidelio subplot suffered the greatest damage in the slashing that reduced *Fidelio* from three acts to two. In the original, this romantic triangle slowed the opera down considerably, so the revisions make Marsellina's and Jacquino's roles significantly less important. In the final *Fidelio*, the subplot makes its appearance only at the beginning and then is almost completely forgotten, serving merely as a vehicle to introduce Fidelio onto the scene.

Nonetheless, this first scene is fascinating as an example — virtually the only one — of how Beethoven might have sounded had he decided to follow more closely in Mozart's operatic footsteps. Beethoven studied Mozart's operas very carefully — there are reverberations from *Così fan tutte*, *Don Giovanni*, *The Marriage of Figaro* and *The Magic Flute* in *Fidelio* — and was able to mimic his master quite closely. Notice the two occasions when a knocking at the jail door interrupts Jacquino's pursuit of Marsellina. This knocking at the gate is reminiscent of the same action in *Macbeth* and serves the same artistic purpose: a portent of fateful events to come.

Jacquino exits and Marsellina sings an aria pouring out her love for Fidelio. The opera has gotten off to an odd start, or so it seems. A dark, violent story of vengeance and liberation begins in the playful style of an eighteenth-century farce. There probably was a point to this opening comedy of manners that has been lost in the successive revisions of *Fidelio*. The false love of Marsellina and Fidelio — false because Fidelio doesn't really exist — was a contrast to the true passion of Leonora and Florestan; one serves to remind us of the other.

Marsellina finishes, and her father, Rocco, enters asking for Fidelio, in a scene that is spoken rather than sung. Then Leonora/Fidelio appears, appropriately enough carrying chains she has just had repaired. It is an unusual entrance for the main character of the opera — in disguise and speaking rather than singing — but a longer, more balanced opening to the opera was jettisoned in the 1806 revision to get us into the action more quickly.

However, all dramatic problems are banished in the musical radiance of the next number, a quartet for Marsellina, Leonora, Rocco and Jacquino. In an instant, the playful quality of the opening is replaced by a mood of beautiful serenity and heartfelt emotion. To a slow, burnished accompaniment in the lower strings, each character in turn discloses his or her feelings at this point in the story. Marsellina is occupied with her love, Leonora consumed with the dangers awaiting her, Rocco happily convinced Fidelio and Marsellina are ready to marry, and Jacquino aghast at the developing romance between the stranger and his former sweetheart.

The quartet is written in the form of a canon, a more sophisticated form of a round such as "Row, Row, Row Your Boat." Marsellina sings her first phrase, which is repeated by Leonora as Marsellina goes on to her second. When Rocco enters with his version of the aria's first phrase, Leonora is on its second phrase and Marsellina on its third, and so on through Jacquino's entry. With each successive character, the accompaniment becomes richer and more expressive, until a simple coda ends this perfect miniature.

Usually in an operatic quartet of this kind, each character is given a different line to sing, reflecting his or her emotions. In departing from this pattern and having each character sing essentially the same music, Beethoven is making a different musical and emotional point. Starting with a single voice, he shows us how the tissue of human emotion and its complications is built up by successive layers of feeling, all of which are essentially the same. We are connected by the similarity of our emotions as well as torn apart by them. The formal beauty of this quartet — one of Beethoven's great slow movements — is an expression of that connectedness.

After the quartet, Rocco embraces Fidelio as his future son-in-law and sings an aria in praise of money and its pleasures. This practical advice was cut in 1806 but restored by Beethoven in 1814. He wanted this down-to-earth moment in his opera to balance its more exalted ones.

Fidelio appeals to Rocco to allow him into the dungeons. Impossible, says Rocco; no one is permitted to visit the political prisoners. Marsellina reminds Rocco of his advancing age, and he relents, but insists that Fidelio may not venture near the mysterious prisoner, two years in chains, who has just had his rations reduced and is near death.

This first hint of Florestan's existence gives Leonora a rush of courage, and in the trio that ends the opera's first scene, she sings of her new resolve (her first real aria so far), while Rocco and Marsellina comment on her courage. Mozart had perfected these closing scenes, which provide plot information as well as musical continuity. Again Beethoven proves himself a good pupil in this adaptation of a familiar Mozartian device. The motivations of the three characters are expressed in different musical lines that nonetheless combine to create a complete whole.

A bright military march announces the arrival of Don Pizarro and his officers and introduces the second scene of act 1. Notice the subtle way Beethoven suggests the bogus nature of Pizarro's claim to military honor. The march keeps stubbornly skipping a beat. Try tapping your foot to it; you'll constantly be out of step.

With the arrival of Don Pizarro, the Arcadian comedy of manners that has characterized *Fidelio* up to now disappears, never to return. From here to its end, *Fidelio* tightens and untightens a continuous spiral of dramatic tension.

Pizarro is a character of unmediated evildoing. Ambitious and ruthless, he would be a cardboard figure of melodrama were it not for the added dimension Beethoven gives him through his music. Pizarro must provide a threatening presence as a foil for Leonora's courage and Florestan's noble suffering. He needs to be larger than life.

As he enters the scene, Pizarro reads a letter that warns him that Don Fernando is planning a surprise visit to the prison the next day to inspect the political prisoners. This visit will uncover Pizarro's treachery in detaining Florestan. He resolves to have Florestan killed that night as his final act of vengeance. A drumroll introduces a truly chilling aria in which Pizarro virtually shouts out his defiance: "Triumph! Victory is mine!" There is more than a touch of the heroic amorality of Don Giovanni in this wild song of revenge. With this single aria, Beethoven creates an atmosphere of total malevolence.

In a duet with Rocco, Pizarro tries to get the old man to agree to kill the mysterious prisoner in chains. Rocco refuses, so Pizarro decides to do the deed himself. He orders Rocco to immediately begin digging a grave for Florestan.

Leonora enters. She has overheard Rocco's and Pizarro's deadly conversation and soliloquizes a response, beginning with a recitative (a sort of musical conversation), which dramatically contrasts Pizarro's evil rage with her mercy. The 1814 revision juxtaposed these portraits of the opera's two protagonists, and Beethoven makes the most of them. Listen to Beethoven's word painting in this recitative, as Leonora pits Pizarro's "wild fury" against "the call of pity, the voice of humanity": "Yet though like ocean billows anger and wrath are raging in your soul, a rainbow shines on me . . . that looks down so quietly, so peacefully." This recitative and the following aria combine to provide Beethoven's first real picture of his heroine, and it is a revealing one.

Beethoven wrote into Leonora his notion of the ideal woman, a feminine presence he had perhaps seen in Helene von Breuning in Bonn (whose daughter was named Eleonore) but had sought in vain ever since. Leonora is passionate and fearless, full of love for one man and humanity both. She is the feminine counterpart of the musical hero Beethoven had just created in the *Eroica*, but here the heroism is wise and loving, born of a strength composed of deep feeling and profound understanding. In 1805, when Beethoven first composed *Fidelio*, he was still searching for such a woman. By 1814, when *Fidelio* was revised, he had found her — his "Immortal Beloved" — but their relationship had been cut short. There is thus great poignancy in Beethoven's idealized sketch of feminine virtue. He is a bit like Pygmalion, creating a perfect character in music to sing to him alone.

Leonora's big aria is accompanied by four horns (actually, three horns and a bassoon) and orchestra. This unusual device perfectly clothes Leonora in the musical garb in which Beethoven imagines her: heroic, almost Amazonian, ready to march into battle against the forces represented by Pizarro. Leonora's aria itself is divided into three sections. The first, lyrical and passionate, contains a universal message: "Come, Hope, let the last star not fade from the weary! Oh come illuminate my goal; however far off, love will attain it." Next, Leonora expresses her resolve in a section introduced by a flourish from the horns: "I shall follow the inner urge, I shall not waver." The music intensifies with her growing confidence, and she begins the last section of the aria, a remembrance of Florestan himself: "O you for whom I have borne everything." Her defiance is a perfect match for Pizarro's.

Leonora's stirring last note has hardly faded before Beethoven adds the final piece to the emotional complex of *Fidelio*. Leonora, seeing Rocco enter, reminds him of a promise long made: to allow the prisoners a chance to leave their cells for a moment and come into the fresh air of the garden. Emboldened by his knowledge of Pizarro's murderous plans, Rocco puts aside his fear of the governor and allows the request. Leonora and Jacquino unlock the cells and retire as the prisoners slowly make their way up to a temporary freedom.

The "Prisoners' Chorus" that follows is one of the best-known passages in *Fidelio*, Beethoven's first chance in the opera to sing a hymn to freedom. The prisoners begin their chorus tentatively, almost inaudibly, before rising to an impassioned celebration of liberty in all its manifestations. The action of the opera is suspended for this moment, and the music is more symphonic than operatic. Twenty years later, Beethoven would again represent the joy of freedom in the chorale finale to his Ninth Symphony, which is strongly foreshadowed in this deeply moving scene.

The chorus is interrupted by a scene between Leonora and Rocco. The old man tells her that Pizarro has approved Marsellina and Fidelio's marriage and has also given permission for Fidelio to accompany Rocco into the dungeon cells. Leonora is overjoyed, until Rocco informs her of the role the two of them must play in the impending murder of the prisoner, who Leonora is now convinced is Florestan. Marsellina and Jacquino rush in to inform Rocco that Pizarro is furious about the release of the prisoners. Pizarro enters, orders the prisoners locked up again and reminds Rocco of their rendezvous in the dungeon. As the prisoners return to their cells in a reprise of their chorus, the remaining characters sing of their respective feelings. Quietly, as the last cell is relocked, the first act of *Fidelio* comes to a close.

The intensity of the first act is redoubled in the second, which opens in a dark underground dungeon, a symbolic representation of the pain of captivity. Originally, the entire act was performed in this gloomy, Freudian setting, although for the 1814 version, the finale was moved aboveground. Even so, the dungeon's fearful darkness creates the dominant mood of the act.

By the opening of act 2, we have been introduced to all the major characters except one. Now we see Florestan for the first time, chained to the wall of his filthy underground cell. Florestan is another of Beethoven's self-portraits, this time the suffering individual in need of rescue and redemption. As we know from the Heiligenstadt Testament, Beethoven was a man familiar with despair. In the character of Florestan we hear that despair in music. Florestan's first words in the opera might be Beethoven's: "God! How dark it is here! This ghastly silence!"

Beethoven announces the mood of act 2 with a mini-overture full of ghostly chords in the brass and heavy-labored heartbeats in the strings. Florestan's opening "Gott!" is an extraordinary cry from the heart, setting the tone of the aria. In Florestan, the horror of lost freedom is given a personal face, in contrast to the anonymous band of prisoners we saw in act 1. Beethoven's measured aria is designed to invoke sympathy for a man who, deprived of all that is important to him, still retains his dignity.

Halfway through the aria, however, the music changes character as Florestan begins to think of Leonora. His longing intensifies, and the music, by constantly changing keys, simulates a form of madness. Listen for Florestan's repeated cries of "Freiheit" (freedom). Exhausted, he sinks to the floor of his cell.

Rocco and Leonora enter to begin a wonderful scene combining spoken dialogue and music. In the darkness, Leonora desperately attempts to get a look at the prisoner. As Rocco begins digging the grave, the music mimics his action, providing an atmospheric counterpart to the scene. Listen especially for the trombones Beethoven introduces into this orchestral texture to suggest malevolence and suspense.

Leonora's emotion increases as she gets closer to the prisoner. Before she actually sees his face, she vows she will free him. Florestan awakes, and Leonora recognizes his voice. He asks for something to drink and Rocco gives him a little wine.

From this point on, almost all the action is set to music, and you may want to listen to the next few scenes a couple of times to fully appreciate them. One time through, try to follow only the dialogue. Another time, just enjoy the music. Eventually you will be able to follow story and music simultaneously.

As Rocco gives Florestan his wine, the three characters on stage — Leonora, Florestan and Rocco — begin a beautiful trio. Florestan thanks his jailers for their act of kindness and hopes he may win them over; Leonora realizes her moment of action is approaching; and Rocco tells us he despises all cruelty. Unlike the quartet in act 1, when all characters sang the same musical line, here each part is different, matching the thoughts and emotions it is intended to express.

Rocco gives the signal to the disguised Pizarro to enter Florestan's cell, and the opera reaches its dramatic height. Pizarro reveals himself to Florestan and advances on him with a dagger. Leonora rushes to protect Florestan. "He must be punished," screams Pizarro. "First kill his wife," cries Leonora, as she reveals her true identity at the opera's climactic point. Pizarro turns on Leonora; she holds him at bay with a pistol. At the height of this action (all set to intensely dramatic music), a trumpet sounds, announcing the arrival of Don Fernando, the minister come to investigate the prison and Pizarro. This trumpet blast, at once representing divine and earthly salvation, signals a crucial element in the philosophical world of *Fidelio*. The opera is not just about personal heroism and a woman's love for her husband, it is about the restoration of earthly order and the triumph of light over darkness in society. The good prince — the ideal Enlightenment ruler — was an essential part of Beethoven's conception of freedom. As much as posterity has wanted to turn him into a revolutionary romantic artist, always ready to value the individual at the expense of society, Beethoven never deserted the Enlightenment ideals he had adopted as a young man. He believed in the possibility of a worldly paradise — a society founded on justice and mercy, to be made on earth by its men and women.

With the arrival of Don Fernando, Pizarro and Rocco hurry away, leaving Leonora and Florestan alone on stage to sing a love duet, "O namenlose Freude!" (O unutterable bliss!), which shocked its original audiences with its delirious passion. Husband and wife have been reunited, and the scene is set for the opera's finale and Florestan's deliverance.

Originally, the final scene of the opera took place within Florestan's cell, with Don Fernando dispensing his justice then and there. However, for the 1814 version, the director of the Viennese opera house decided to set the liberation scene in the courtyard of the jail, necessitating an unfortunate break in the action. To cover this scene change, sometimes the overture to the 1806 production, now called *Leonora* no. 3, is played at this point, as it features the same trumpet call that we have just heard in the opera and thus acts as a replay of Florestan's rescue. Sometimes the audience just waits.

The finale to *Fidelio* is almost like another opera in miniature. All the threads of the plot come together in a joyous outburst remarkably reminiscent of the finale of the Ninth Symphony. The action begins with Don Fernando freeing the prisoners, accompanied by a martial flourish in C major, the most basic and fundamental of keys. Fernando pardons the prisoners with Enlightenment noblesse: ". . . that I may lift the night of crime which has shrouded all in heavy blackness."

The music changes character, and Rocco comes forward to tell the story of Florestan and Leonora. Fernando is amazed, having believed Florestan dead, and arrests Pizarro. The music changes again, and Fernando allows Leonora to remove Florestan's chains. As they fall away, a quick modulation opens up a sweet strain in the winds as Leonora and Florestan embrace.

Finally, full chorus and soloists propel the music to an excited conclusion that again prefigures the choral finale of the Ninth Symphony. "Anyone who has a fair wife of his own, join in our rejoicing! Our song can never praise too highly the rescue of her husband."

Beethoven never wrote another opera after *Fidelio*, although he considered and rejected dozens of librettos. His one musical drama, therefore, has taken on an unusual significance, the sole theatrical statement of a master of musical suspense. *Fidelio* succeeds almost entirely because of the sublime power of Beethoven's music, which turns what could have been a forgettable melodrama into a timeless statement of the joy of freedom. To listen to *Fidelio* is to be reminded that the ideals of liberty and optimism were once bright and young in human history and that Beethoven lived in that dawn. The care that Beethoven lavished on his opera, first in 1805, then for the 1806 revision, then again for the 1814 revision, demonstrates that this was no ordinary composition for him but an important summation of his personal philosophy. It was a philosophy Beethoven had begun to form in Bonn at the end of the eighteenth century but which now, in the middle of the first decade of the nineteenth, had come to animate all his music. Finally Beethoven was able to express everything he had long felt and contemplated in his art.

11

The Summer of a Life

T he decade ushered in at Heiligenstadt, the decade of the *Eroica* and *Fidelio*, saw Beethoven at his most remarkably productive. He had fulfilled his dream: to be the "great man" he had felt himself destined to become ten years earlier, an artist setting off on an independent path, increasingly subject to no law but his own. For several years he strode through his musical world without a false move, writing with an assurance that was not shaken by his deafness nor his sometimes hostile reception by the Viennese public. Beethoven's certainty about his musical path struck some as arrogant. A British musician and publisher, Muzio Clementi, referred to him as "that haughty beauty" when he was negotiating a contract with him; Haydn had for years only half-jokingly called Beethoven "our Grand Mogul."

In this first decade of the nineteenth century, Beethoven produced a stream of masterpieces that still remain the heart of the Western classical repertoire: Symphonies no. 3 through 8, his Fourth and Fifth Piano Concertos, the three *Razumovsky* String Quartets, a violin concerto, the *Waldstein* and *Appassionata* Piano Sonatas, *Fidelio*, and many more compositions. In every field he touched, he set the standard for generations to come, honing a musical language that became more concentrated and more powerful with each successive work. This is Beethoven's "second period," his "heroic decade." Perhaps fifteen of the twenty most popular classical pieces ever written by anyone came from Beethoven's pen during this one decade — an amazing achievement.

Everything we associate with Beethoven today is concentrated in these "heroic" works. They overflow with sentiment and personal meaning, speaking with a voice that seems at once deeply passionate and intensely powerful. Blessed with a natural simplicity, they still continue to amaze with the wealth of their musical ideas. (Beethoven was one of the most imaginative composers in Western musical history, in addition to all his other strengths.) Most of all, they stake out for music its claim to be the most sublime of the arts, a means of expressing the inexpressible For listeners, they are the pinnacle of Beethoven's achievements, the high point of his creative life that still stands unshadowed today. Coming into contact with these masterpieces remains a thrilling and illuminating experience.

Where had this music come from? One source was certainly deep within Beethoven's own personality. We can trace the emergence of his mature style to the interior battles he waged with his personal demons, those associated with his family and his health. The Beethoven we hear in this music is an individual confronting his own weaknesses in a spirit of defiance, and triumphing over them.

But Beethoven's mature achievement had a social as well as a psychological source. In 1770, when Beethoven was born, the status of musicians had not changed greatly since the twelfth and thirteenth centuries, when they were nothing more than vassals of a feudal lord. By his death, musicians held an essentially modern position as freelance artists. This fundamental change in the economics of music making had more than a financial impact on Beethoven and his contemporaries. No longer able to count on the security of a guaranteed place in an aristocratic court, musicians were now obligated to present themselves to the public as self-sufficient artists, dependent on nothing but their talent for their success. As well, the growth of music publishing and public performance was creating an international musical public, anonymous and middle-class, to replace the cozy salon gatherings at which Beethoven had begun his career.

Although Beethoven was never entirely freed from his ties to aristocratic patrons (by choice as much as by necessity), the new institutions of music making helped push him to develop his mature musical style. He was now able, even obliged, to conceive his music as a free response to the world he perceived around and within him. No longer enclosed within a strict social stratum, Beethoven could address the world as a single individual, defining himself solely by his power as an artist. It was a liberation for which he had prepared himself for a decade.

The works of Beethoven's heroic decade are thus his most public, conceived on a grand scale and constantly seeking the new. A musician of a princely court could be successful churning out variations on the same theme year after year. The changed musical climate of the early nineteenth century, however, demanded that each new work be different, and strikingly so. Beethoven happily complied, and seldom repeated himself. The Third Symphony (*Eroica*) had been a massive, powerful work. His Fourth, composed two years later, was more intimate. The monumental Fifth Symphony was composed and premiered at the same time as the pastoral Sixth. The Seventh and Eighth, also composed together, contrasted extremes of demonic ribaldry and domestic calm.

The originality and novelty of Beethoven's works made them highly controversial. Many were greeted with puzzled bewilderment by large portions of the Viennese and European public, despite their fame. The initial reviews of the *Eroica* were mixed; *Fidelio* was a failure in its original production and didn't fare much better when it was revised and remounted several months later. The *Razumovsky* Quartets were especially reviled, considered "a patchwork by a madman." One Russian musician was so enraged by them that he ripped his part from the music stand and stomped all over it. Even the original performers, for whom the music had been written, were so taken aback by some of the novelties in the score that they were convinced Beethoven was playing a joke on them.

Beethoven remained unperturbed by these negative reactions. He told his friend Ignaz Schuppanzigh, who had complained of the *Razumovskys*, "They are not for you, but for the ages." Nor did the controversy harm his public image. If anything, it increased Beethoven's fame and added to his reputation as a heroic, masterful musician ready to put aside public acclaim to remain true to his artistic vision. For all those who lamented the "willful eccentricities" in Beethoven's works — that is, those passages that stray from the traditional and consequently demand more attention — there were as many who considered them conclusive proof of Beethoven's genius and revered him for them.

More so now than at any other time, Beethoven's life was almost totally concentrated on his music. He had been something of a slow starter as a composer, but now produced one composition after another, each more exalted than its predecessor. When he wasn't writing his music, he was arranging to have it printed and performed. He spent months in negotiations with publishers throughout Europe to get the best terms for his works. Musicians in those days were also expected to arrange for their own concerts, and Beethoven was forced to attend to the most tedious details of his occasional public displays. For his *Akademie* (concert) of December 22, 1808 — a four-hour affair in a freezing ballroom — Beethoven conducted the first performances of both the Fifth and Sixth Symphonies as well as the *Choral Fantasia*, performed the premiere of the Fourth Piano Concerto and improvised on the keyboard. No wonder that for a decade there are almost no references in his correspondence to his deafness or melancholy; his concentration on his work was almost complete.

This is not to say that his personal life was untroubled during these immensely productive years. Increasingly, the great compositions were produced against a background of despair, loneliness and personal disorder. Beethoven's deafness and consequent social isolation continued to fan the flames of mistrust that had long been his constant companion. No friend or associate was immune from bursts of the terrible Beethovian temper. Stephan von Breuning, Beethoven's childhood friend who had joined him in Vienna and worked with him on the revisions to *Fidelio*, painted this portrait of the composer in a letter to Franz Wegeler in late 1804:

> You cannot conceive, my dear Wegeler, what an indescribable, I might say, fearful effect the gradual loss of his hearing has had upon him. Think of the feeling of being unhappy in one of such violent temperament: in addition reservedness, mistrust, often toward his best friends, in many things want of decision! For the greater part, with only an occasional exception when he gives free vent to his feelings on the spur of the moment, intercourse with him is a real exertion, at which one can scarcely trust to oneself.

Breuning knew whereof he spoke. A minor dispute over an unpaid month's rent at the flat they shared had caused a split between them that lasted for over a year, during which time they never exchanged a word. And this was hardly an isolated incident. A waiter in Beethoven's favorite restaurant who once brought him the wrong dish had it thrown back in his face. Friends of years standing were banished for the slightest misdemeanor. Ries was astonished one day to see Beethoven and his brother Carl come to blows in the street. As he aged, Beethoven's control over himself weakened, just as his control over his art strengthened. He was, as Goethe was to later remark, "an utterly untamed personality."

Beethoven himself was painfully aware of the violence of his temper. His correspondence is full of abject apologies begging for-giveness for his outbursts. Nonetheless, he seemed powerless to con-trol his behavior and was especially susceptible to slanderous statements made to him about his closest friends. His enemies knew that a whispered word here or there impugning an associate would always have Beethoven believing the worst. Invariably, Beethoven would abandon those he needed most, only to discover his mistake after the damage had been done.

Beethoven's impetuousness had serious consequences. So abusive was his behavior during rehearsals that several orchestras refused to play for him, preventing him on more than one occasion from mount-ing the public concerts that were a major source of his income. In the summer of 1806, his major patron, Prince Lichnowsky, then paying Beethoven a handsome yearly honorarium, insisted just a bit too forcefully for the composer's liking that he play for some French offi-cers. Not only did Beethoven refuse to play, he stomped out of the prince's summer palace, walked home to Vienna in a violent storm and smashed a bust of Lichnowsky to pieces. The honorarium proba-bly ceased soon thereafter. At its worst, Beethoven's volatility verged on cruelty and self-destructiveness.

At the same time, Beethoven was capable of remarkable kindness and generosity. Except for a couple of instances, he never failed Ferdinand Ries, taking him on as a pupil despite his notorious aver-sion to teaching. Besides feeling a genuine affection for Ries, the com-poser never forgot that his pupil's father had helped the Beethoven household in Bonn. There are other stories. When a gifted pianist and friend of Beethoven's, Dorothea von Ertmann, lost a child, says Ries, "Beethoven at first did not want to come into the house; at length he invited her to visit him, and when she came he sat himself down at the pianoforte and said simply: 'We will now talk to each other in tones,' and for an hour played without stopping, and as she remarked: 'He told me everything, and at last brought me comfort.'" Nor was this an isolated incident. To console the often ill and melancholy Antonie Brentano, a woman Beethoven may well have loved, he would enter the anteroom to her bedroom, play for an hour or so and leave without otherwise announcing his presence. Ries, who knew Beethoven as well as anyone during these years, recognized the contradictions in his teacher's personality yet nevertheless concluded: "On the whole Beethoven was a thoroughly good and kind man, on whom his moods and impetuousness played shabby tricks. He would have forgiven anybody, no matter how grievously he had injured him or whatever wrong he had done him, if he had found him in an unfortunate position."

Beethoven's isolation from society, exacerbated by his deafness, meant that he led a daily life of increasing disorder. A bachelor now in his mid-thirties, Beethoven began to neglect the mundane details of day-to-day life in his single-minded concentration on his art. He paid less and less attention to his dress, wandering through Vienna in whatever clothes were immediately at hand. Despite the best efforts of a long string of servants, with whom Beethoven was constantly at war, his lodgings were chaotic. Depending on his whim, Beethoven might eat or not eat, sleep or not sleep, dress or not dress. He was a man utterly unregulated in his personal habits.

This domestic squalor shocked the few in Vienna who knew of it. In 1809, when Napoleon's armies were occupying Vienna for a second time, Baron de Trémont, a French aristocrat who greatly admired Beethoven's music, went out of his way to meet his idol. He described to a friend the incredible scene that met him as he entered Beethoven's flat:

> Picture to yourself the extreme of dirt and disorder: pools of water decorating the floor; and a rather ancient grand piano on which dust competed for room with sheets of written or printed notes. Under it — I do not exaggerate — an unemptied

chamber pot. . . . Most of the chairs had straw seats and were decorated with clothes and with dishes full of the remains of the previous day's supper.

Marriage might have been an answer, but Beethoven does not seem to have pursued the possibility at this time, when his powers were at their height. However, he was often in love. In the late 1790s, he formed perhaps his first great attachment, with a young noble-woman named Giulietta Guicciardi, to whom he dedicated the *Moonlight* Sonata. The affair with Giulietta seems to have been deeply passionate, but in 1803 she suddenly married another composer and dropped out of Beethoven's life.

Soon after, in the winter of 1803–04, Beethoven became deeply involved with another young woman he had first met in 1799. Josephine Brunsvik, now Josephine Deym, was Giulietta's cousin and by all accounts a great beauty. Beethoven had been interested in Josephine when she had come to Vienna as a girl of nineteen and he was engaged to give her piano lessons. Her family, however, decided that a Count Deym, thirty years Josephine's senior, would make her a good match, and she was married in 1801. The marriage was a disaster, although the couple produced three children. When Deym died in 1804, just after the birth of their fourth child, Josephine suffered a severe breakdown. Within a few months Beethoven's interest in her had been rekindled, and they clearly fell in love, much to the alarm of Josephine's family.

The Beethoven of 1804 must have cut a curious figure as a suitor. His deafness would have made him a difficult, if not impossible, choice as a husband, and the domestic turmoil in which he surrounded himself was simply unredeemable. More to the point, Beethoven could never be considered a suitable husband for a child of the nobility like Giulietta Guicciardi or Josephine Brunsvik-Deym. His prospects were uncertain, his family connections nil. Beethoven was a commoner, and the women he was attracted to were invariably aristocrats. As much as Beethoven might have erased these distinctions in his art and wanted to erase them in his life, they were still a powerful force in society, especially the society in which Beethoven felt most at home. It would have taken an extraordinary woman to renounce her position to marry Beethoven and plunge into his passionate but disordered world. Later, as we shall see, Beethoven did meet such a woman, but Josephine was not the one.

It wasn't that Beethoven did not fascinate Josephine and other women; he clearly did. To the right woman, a soul that could produce such wonderful music would always be appealing. However, for Josephine the appeal had its limits, as she tried to explain to the composer in a letter she drafted but never sent.

> The closer relationship with you, dear Beethoven, these winter months has left impressions in my heart which neither time — nor circumstances — will erase. . . . My soul, already inspired about you before I knew you personally has been nourished by your affection. A feeling that lies deep in my soul and is incapable of expression made me love you; even before I knew you your music aroused inspiration within me — your kind nature and your affection strengthened it. The favor which you have accorded me, the pleasure of your company would have been the finest ornament of my life if you had been able to love me less sensuously — that I cannot satisfy this sensuous love — does this cause you anger — I would have to break holy vows were I to listen to your desire — Believe me — it is I through the fulfillment of my duty who suffer the most — and my actions have been surely dictated by noble motives.

Romantic disappointments were not Beethoven's only problem in the years when he was creating his most powerful masterpieces; he also had money troubles. Beethoven's rocky relationships with his patrons and his irregular income from published works made financial security a mere dream. And even though the poverty of his Bonn days constantly haunted him, Beethoven was terrible with money, spending it freely and lavishly when it came his way, his impulsive nature rendering financial planning impossible. Beethoven hated haggling with his publishers and all his life sought an exclusive arrangement by which he would offer all his works to a single firm for an agreed-upon price. Beethoven did negotiate such a deal with Muzio Clementi for the sale of his works in Great Britain but never could establish a similar relationship with a Viennese publisher.

Then, in 1808, when Beethoven was working on the Fifth and Sixth Symphonies, an opportunity arose that seemed to offer a solution to his financial problems. Jerome Bonaparte, Napoleon's brother, having been installed as prince of Westphalia, invited Beethoven to come to his court in Cassel as *Kapellmeister*. Unexpectedly, Beethoven expressed interest, despite the fact that the office of *Kapellmeister* was something of an anachronism in 1808, two decades after the French Revolution. As well, it seemed inconceivable that one of Europe's most famous composers would imprison himself in a tiny provincial capital when all of Europe lay at his feet. Nonetheless, the documents were drawn up, ready for the composer's signature.

At that moment, in early 1809, the nobility of Vienna roused themselves to head off what would certainly have been seen as a major international embarrassment. Three aristocrats — the archduke Rudolph, Beethoven's pupil, as well as the princes Lobkowitz and Kinsky — jointly agreed to pay Beethoven an annual salary of 4,000 florins on the sole condition that he remain in Vienna. At last, Beethoven had achieved his long-desired security, and in a form that would have been unthinkable only a decade before. The contract symbolized a new relationship between patron and composer. No longer was the musician to serve the prince and receive a stipend in return; now the prince was to serve the musician. In the words of the contract:

> The daily proofs which Herr Ludwig van Beethoven is giving
> of his extraordinary talents and genius as musician and com-
> poser, awaken the desire that he surpass the great expectations
> which are justified by his past achievements. But as it has been
> demonstrated that only one who is as free from care as possible
> can devote himself to a single department of activity and create
> works of magnitude which are exalted and which ennoble
> art, the undersigned have decided to place Herr Ludwig van
> Beethoven in a position where the necessaries of life shall
> not cause him embarrassment or clog his powerful genius.

The annuity contract was the most powerful acknowledgment Beethoven had yet received of the impact his music had made on his contemporaries. His decade of masterpieces had cemented his reputation in nineteenth-century Vienna as it has formed the basis of his popularity ever since. In a mere fifteen years, Beethoven had moved from the tentative student of Haydn to the master of his craft, an artistic giant who had discovered a power in music none imagined possible. To experience any one of these mature works is to feel the force of his personality at its strongest.

12

The Heroic Style:
The *Appassionata* Sonata

Hardly any music ever written seems to need explaining less than the masterpieces of Beethoven's heroic period. These works still speak directly and powerfully to us with a perfection that seems to defy analysis. What is important to listen for in these works is not so much their musical energy — who could ignore that? — but the subtle simplicity with which Beethoven creates his effects. Because, of course, the sense of simple inevitability that characterizes these works comes from sophisticated musical thinking. The heroic works present a unique amalgam of careful craft and overwhelming emotion. To see the two at work together is to understand the essence of Beethoven's technique. Beethoven the passionate rationalist unfolds in these works.

Beethoven discovered the power of the orchestra during his heroic decade. Many of the great compositions of the decade are orchestral — the big symphonies and the famous concertos. But the style was every bit as effective for chamber music or for solo piano. Beethoven learned to treat the smaller forces as though they were miniature orchestras.

Thus we're going to use the *Appassionata* Piano Sonata, op. 57 — one of Beethoven's most famous compositions — as our guide to his heroic style. Written in 1804 and 1805, only a year after the *Eroica*, the *Appassionata* typifies the language Beethoven used throughout his heroic period. Beethoven learned to fit more and more musical information into smaller and smaller spaces, compressing its energy like a tightly coiled spring. The simplest materials become packed with a sort of nuclear power ready to explode when released. If there is a single thread unifying all the second-period compositions, it is this reliance on minute musical means to make a large impact.

We're going to look at the entire *Appassionata* in this chapter, our first complete work since *Für Elise*. It is almost impossible to divide the middle-period works into single movements, so carefully did Beethoven tie all of them together. Not only did he use similar motifs and ideas throughout his compositions, he began to fuse movements together so that the motive power of one would flow without interruption into the next. He used this technique for the first time in linking the second and third movements of the *Appassionata*, and then liked the effect so much he repeated it in the Fifth Symphony and the *Emperor* Piano Concerto.

The *Appassionata* is in sonata form but with an interesting twist. As Beethoven increased the emotional power of his middle-period works, their form became not larger and more complicated but shorter and simpler. The first movement of the *Eroica* had an immense and complicated structure whose power depended on its size. In his middle works, Beethoven managed to keep the power of the *Eroica* while returning to the proportions of his earliest work. Rather than expanding horizontally, becoming larger and longer, the works expanded vertically, becoming deeper and more intense. Let's turn to the *Appassionata* to see this increasing power at work.

As we've come to expect, the character of the first movement of the *Appassionata* is set right from the beginning by its opening theme. It is a dramatic and mysterious theme, a triad that first descends, pauses, then ascends the keyboard, finishing off with a little trill. It is played very softly in the deeper recesses of the bass, as though we were still in the dungeons of *Fidelio*. Whereas many of Beethoven's earlier themes had been emotionally neutral, the better to develop later, the theme of the *Appassionata* has a very definite character. Beethoven plunges us instantly into a dark and dramatic world. Although it is a dangerous game to impute extra-musical associations to purely instrumental music, this theme and the rest of the sonata constantly echo with the sounds of war and the intimation of death.

The theme is then repeated with one critical difference. The second time through, it is played a semitone higher. The impact of this simple device is quite profound. Since all the notes of the second version are different from those of the first, Beethoven can instantly add a new accent and character to the music while staying firmly within the opening musical pattern: maximum impact with minimum means. He can also momentarily disrupt our expectations. We don't normally change harmonies in a sonata without a few hints via a transition passage. Here Beethoven has changed key (if just for a second) completely without warning. Remember that transposition of a semitone. As innocent as it may seem, it will become one of the major musical ideas of the entire sonata — all three movements — providing the work with an unheard-of unity.

Beethoven returns to his original key to replay the last half of the first theme (a technique we've seen him use before), and there again is that semitone, this time in the bass, sounding like an ominous drumroll. Pay attention to that drumroll: this little idea is one of the key building blocks of the movement. The right hand tries to develop the main idea, always to be interrupted by the fateful summons of that four-note left-hand figure. The right hand finally capitulates, mimicking the rhythm of the left. The drumroll continues. Finally, an explosive figure — marked "forte" — cascades down the keyboard, and the music comes to a halt.

All this has taken fifty seconds and a mere fifteen bars. But through the use of dynamics, pauses, obsessively repeated figures and simple ideas, Beethoven has packed a tremendous amount of musical drama into this small space. Gone is the leisurely expansion of a theme that had characterized the *Eroica*. Here everything is gestural, terse, pregnant with meaning.

After the pause, the main theme begins again but is interrupted by an explosive outburst of chords that stop it in its tracks. It continues, only to be interrupted a second time, continues again and is interrupted again. This is a highly effective passage in which Beethoven manages to develop his theme without ever leaving it, providing deep emotional contrast with the simplest of means.

After the third outburst, the music is finally allowed to continue in a spare passage characterized by a constantly repeated note in the left hand (an echo of the opening drumroll figure). We noted the claustrophobic effect of a repeated note when we looked at *Für Elise*. No matter how much the music wishes to wander, the repeated note forces it to stay in one place. However, here, while the music sounds anchored, it is actually changing key and moving toward the *b* section of the exposition.

The change of character in the accompaniment to a soft rolling wave is the clue that Beethoven has entered the second-theme area in the *Appassionata*. The first-theme section of the movement has been very short — only thirty-four bars, similar to the proportions of op. 2, no. 1 — but its emotional impact has been intense. We now need a change of pace, the kind a second theme is supposed to provide.

And we get it. The minor key of the first theme changes to a softer major for the second, and a new emotional character — warmer and more open — is immediately introduced. Once again Beethoven manages to fit drama firmly within the confines of standard sonata form.

The emotional counterpoint between first and second themes in the *Appassionata* is one of Beethoven's most dramatic. The deep resonance of the second theme, with its powerful rising octaves, could not provide a more pointed contrast to the nervous, macabre energy of the first. However, from a musical point of view the two ideas are remarkably similar, like a set of twins, one malevolent, one beatific. Sing the two themes over to yourself to see the connection. The rhythm of the two ideas is almost the same, and although the direction of the melodies is different, they are both made up of broken triads, almost carbon copies of one another. Here is that primary feature of middle-period Beethoven, his ability to convey the broadest possible emotion with the fewest possible means. Each note or phrase carries a weight of musical meanings.

Beethoven replays his second theme a couple of times, but in keeping with the fragmentary quality of this movement ends the theme quite abruptly and introduces a long, snaky chromatic scale in the right hand, which covers the entire keyboard with its sinuous, ambiguous harmony. Then, out of nowhere, a furious series of broken chords erupts in both hands, back in F minor, the key of the first section of the exposition. This bit of musical fireworks is repeated twice and leads into the coda to the exposition, which ends with the first theme returning to the depths of the piano from which it came, like an animal returning to its den.

The exposition of the *Appassionata* is only sixty-five bars long, but it is all Beethoven needed to create the effect he wanted. The expressive themes, the many pauses and the dramatic virtuoso passages all add up to a concentrated musical brew, only a sip of which is highly intoxicating. Gone is the powerful scale of the *Eroica*; in its place this tightly coiled spring of a movement.

There is no repeat of the exposition in this anxious first movement. The quote from the main theme that ended the exposition also serves to begin the development, which starts with a statement of the main theme in E major (a semitone lower than the F minor in which the exposition ended). However, this major-key statement of the theme is treated in the same fragmentary manner as most of the exposition. The closing trill of the theme is played several times as Beethoven gathers steam for the development proper, but the music continues to move at a leisurely pace, with its constant stops and starts. Beethoven is in no hurry to move us along but instead wants to build a sense of anticipation for what is to come in the development.

The E major abruptly changes to E minor, and the first episode of the development takes shape. It will be the longest continuous musical section so far in the movement. The section is organized around the main motif, which is first heard in the bass, then imitated in the treble. The first pattern is in E minor, which modulates (changes key) to C minor for a second repetition of the pattern, then to A-flat major for a third, with a slightly brighter sound to the formula.

Finally, Beethoven writes himself out of this section by having his widely spaced arpeggios cascade toward each other and converge on a single repeated note. And then, in the heart of the development, Beethoven gives us perhaps the last thing we expect: he returns to the pattern of the exposition. This semi-reprise of the exposition is ushered in by that repeated note, which we now remember signaled the transition from first theme to second at the beginning of the piece. Here in the development it serves the same purpose. The harmonies are different, and Beethoven adds a passage or two that was not in the exposition, but we are being led toward the second theme as surely as though this were the recap.

Throughout this passage, we keep expecting this master of surprise to move us to a totally new musical location, but he surprises us most by refusing to do so. The transition passage gives way to a remarkably faithful statement of the second theme. We noted that Beethoven spent very little time in the exposition with that beautiful *b* theme, moving away from it almost as soon as it was introduced. Now he lets us hear it in several harmonic guises, repeating it three complete times.

Once Beethoven exhausts this idea, he changes the mood once again to give us almost a free fantasia in the middle of the sonata.

Rolling arpeggios on a single chord cascade up and then down the keyboard in a virtuoso display that serves to arrest the forward harmonic motion of the music. The intensity of the music, however, increases as the arpeggios growl through the depths of the piano, and Beethoven leads to the climax of the development with the one idea from the exposition he has not yet used: that four-note drumroll motif from the beginning. But where before it had been just an ominous note on the horizon, now it explodes in all its ferocity. Beethoven lived during a generation at war; it doesn't take much imagination to hear the insistent drum beats of conflict in this hammered-out, double-forte conclusion to the development. This is the kind of power only Beethoven has ever put into music: blatant, uncensored, untamed.

The four-note motif finally subsides to a repeated single note in the bass when Beethoven provides another surprise. On top of this incessantly repeated note, Beethoven begins the recapitulation. There, in the right hand, is the main theme, exactly as originally heard. We noted before that the recapitulation was the weak point in the sonata chain, the spot where a too regular return to the opening of a movement could ruin all the drama that had emerged during the development. Here Beethoven solves this problem brilliantly, by having the development, embodied by that single repeating note, carry on right into the recapitulation. It is as though the emotional intensity of the development refuses to end, staying on past the point where it should have disappeared.

And that repeated note is not just heard for a few bars but pounds out through the entire first and second statements of the theme in the recap, providing a riveting and inescapable accompaniment to it. Only a master artist would attempt such a challenging move, daring his audience to accept what borders on ugliness.

The repeated note finally ends with the two chords that close off the first major statement of the theme, and Beethoven is ready for another small surprise. Were he to follow the pattern of his exposition exactly, we would hear the explosive chords in minor that originally accompanied the second statement of the main idea. Beethoven's instincts told him that such a moment in the recap might sound anticlimactic after the drama of the opening statement. So in a single stroke, he changes the minor to major. The effect is electric. With that one alteration, a terrible moment in minor becomes triumphant and exultant in major.

The switch to a major key is only temporary, however, as Beethoven quickly returns to the pattern and proportions of his original. The remainder of the recapitulation is striking for its fidelity to the exposition. Except for the changes necessary to alter the key of the second theme (now in a warm F major to balance the F minor of the first theme), the same themes and transition sections are heard in the same order as in the exposition, with the same emphasis. The recap to the *Appassionata* is one of the most regular Beethoven ever wrote; he knew that he had packed so much tension into the exposition and development that his audience needed formal regularity to readjust their sensibilities.

He also knew he was about to launch into a coda that was very much like a second development. The extended coda had been a part of Beethoven's basic musical language since the *Eroica*. He had come to depend on it for the expansion of form and breadth of musical thought his imagination demanded. More and more this extended coda turned the *aba* format of a sonata movement closer to an *abab* pattern.

This is what Beethoven does here, with a coda that is almost as long as the development and that shares some of the same musical features. It begins with a quote from the first theme, heard first in the home key, then transposed up a semitone for a repeat. This section is repeated with increasing intensity, then leads to a quote of the second theme. First and second themes are finally placed in immediate proximity to one another.

Beethoven replays his second theme several times, getting louder each time, until the music suddenly gives way to an extended passage of broken chords and arpeggios that takes over for a full eighteen bars, a sort of cadenza in the middle of a sonata. This is a technique Beethoven borrowed from the concerto, where at the end of a movement a soloist was permitted free range to perform an extended solo passage before the orchestra reentered. In his desire to bring to the piano sonata more of the texture of the symphony, Beethoven writes his pianist a cadenza, even though there is no orchestra to accompany it.

The passage works because not only does it provide a thrilling moment of technical virtuosity, it also helps build the musical power of the movement. Beethoven has been quite terse up to now in this sonata, and he needs to relax his grip and let soloist and audience revel in sheer sound.

And notice how cleverly Beethoven returns to the world of the sonata as the cadenza closes, with the four-note drumroll motif that acts as a kind of ghostly knock on the door throughout the movement.

That motif is repeated several times before Beethoven speeds up the action and heads the movement home to its close. The drumroll motif sounds double-forte in full chords, and Beethoven launches into a version of his second theme, now in a minor key.

We noted earlier the essential similarity of the first and second themes in this movement, but it is not until this concluding coda that Beethoven makes the most of their likeness. Up to now, he has been careful to present his first theme in a minor key and his second in a major (with a couple of exceptions in the development), so that we can keep them separate. Now, just as the movement is about to close, Beethoven presents the accompaniment figure he used for his second theme in the minor tonality he reserved for his first. For a moment, we don't know which idea, first or second, we're listening to. It is as though Beethoven has re-created here at the very end of the movement the essential unity of his twin themes.

Beethoven increases the intensity of this hybrid idea until the texture gives way to a set of furious chords in both hands (related once again to the drumroll motif). Then the main theme returns, first ascending and finally descending to the depths of the keyboard whence it had come many bars ago. The movement comes to a hushed, deep close.

Although the *Appassionata* belongs to the era inaugurated by the *Eroica* symphony, the two are quite different. The first movement of the *Appassionata* is much shorter than that of the symphony and much more regular in form. The *Eroica*, you will remember, was full of separate musical ideas that Beethoven needed hundreds of bars to finally order. The *Appassionata* has relatively few ideas, and their relation to one another is always quite clear. The formal scheme of the sonata is very simple compared with the sprawling dimensions of the symphony.

Yet it is this very simplicity that allows Beethoven to create the sensational emotion of the *Appassionata*. The musical texture itself — the themes, the virtuoso displays — is so dramatic that its form needs to be simple. Too much attention on the form would dissipate the awful power of the music itself. It was not until the very last years of Beethoven's life, with the Ninth Symphony, that he would combine the intensity of the *Appassionata* with the scale of the *Eroica*.

Clarity of form also characterizes the second movement of the *Appassionata*, a theme and variations. Theme and variations was a form beloved of all the classical masters. A tune (theme) is presented once and then repeated with one element or other of the original changed. Sometimes a major theme is played in minor; sometimes a martial theme is varied as a waltz. Often composers used a good deal of humor in these movements, and they provided entertaining inter-ludes in the midst of a sonata.

Not so in the *Appassionata*. In one of those movements whose secrets seem to defy analysis, Beethoven has managed to build a structure of deepening intensity out of a simple theme and three very simple variations. The stark, turbulent world of the first movement finds its counterpart here in a mood of almost religious contemplation.

The organization of the movement is straightforward. It begins with the theme, which is nothing but a series of simple primary chords, carefully positioned and rhythmically regular. The first half of the theme, which is repeated, is extremely basic; the second half (also repeated) is a little more interesting rhythmically. Together they present a complete contrast to the violence of the first movement and a framework for all of the second.

The first variation follows and it couldn't be simpler. The right hand plays almost exactly the same notes as it did for the theme itself, and the left hand merely displaces its notes by half a beat. Where the two hands had played simultaneously at first, now they are a half-beat apart. Nothing could be simpler, but the effect is wonderful. It is as though the theme has shifted slightly out of focus, splitting into two images. We're never exactly sure which of the two lines we should be listening to, and our ear skips back and forth between them.

Beethoven reverses this technique for the second variation. Now it is the bass line (the left hand) that replays its notes from the theme and the right hand that adds something new — a new line, almost a melody, flowing evenly and continuously through the variation like a beautiful, clear stream. As in the first variation, there is a slight climax in the second half.

For the third variation, that flowing line slyly doubles in speed and becomes the accompaniment for a statement of the theme in chords off the beat. First the chords are in the right hand and the accompaniment in the left; for the repeat of each section, the two hands are reversed.

In his career, Beethoven wrote many sets of variations — some of enormous size, others of intricate sophistication — in which every variation is in a separate key or concentrated on a novel, rich texture. The *Appassionata* variations do nothing of the sort, staying in the same key throughout and hardly ever varying the texture. Yet somehow their power of development is equal to any other set of Beethoven variations. The very simplicity of the changes from one variation to the next allows us to register them in a profound way; we seem to be watching an organic creature grow before our eyes.

As the third variation ends, the movement slows, and the theme returns almost exactly as it was first presented. Beethoven does make a few subtle changes to it, incorporating bits and pieces of the variations to which it was subjected, but the intent is to return us to the security of the theme after the changes of the variations. A sense of deep repose is achieved with the subtlest of effects. The conflict and stress of the first movement seem far behind us.

But they are not. Just as the second movement seems about to come to a close, a dreamy chord interrupts the music, followed by a sharp series of repeated dissonant chords. The peace of the middle movement is to be short-lived. Suddenly the music changes tempo, character and place, and we are plunged into the last movement. This elision of the second and third movements of the *Appassionata* never fails to startle, even when you know it is coming. It allows Beethoven to accentuate the drama of his final musical statement.

The last movement is a *perpetuum mobile*, a whirlwind of music that restores the passionate emotion that dominated the first movement but adds to it a relentless character. The movement is virtually monothematic: one idea constantly repeated makes up its entire texture. That idea is heard right at the beginning of the third movement, after the relentless drumming of the transition section that ends the second. It is a flowing idea that zooms upward on an F-minor triad and then snakes back down:

Ferdinand Ries gives us a glimpse of the very moment when this movement took shape in Beethoven's mind and found its way through his fingers to the keyboard. Ries and Beethoven were in the country in the summer of 1804:

> During [one of our] walk[s] we went so far astray that we didn't get back to Dobling, where Beethoven lived, until nearly eight o'clock. The entire way he had hummed, or sometimes even howled to himself, up and down, up and down, without singing any definite notes. When I asked what this was, he replied: "A theme for the last Allegro of the sonata has occurred to me." When we entered the room he rushed to the piano without taking off his hat. I took a seat in the corner and he soon forgot all about me. He stormed on for at least an hour with the new finale of this sonata, which is so beautiful. Finally he got up, was surprised to see me still there, and said: "I cannot give you a lesson today, I still have work to do."

Although they are carefully concealed, there are many similarities between the opening themes of the first and third movements of the

Appassionata. Both are made up of the notes of the F-minor triad, although in the third movement the notes (obviously played much faster) go up and then down, the opposite of the first-movement pattern. More tellingly, Beethoven repeats in the third movement his technique of raising the theme a semitone for its second repetition. Listen to the beginning of the movement. The main idea is heard twice in the home key, then is repeated twice a half-tone higher. The effect here is the same as in the sonata's beginning. A whole new array of tones is introduced into the piece in the simplest of fashions.

The key to understanding the last movement of the *Appassionata* is following that main theme in its many guises. After its first statement, including the raised half-tone repetition, the whole idea is repeated, this time with brief two-note punctuations in the right hand. Those punctuations then form something of a little melodic idea for the next few bars, with the first few notes of the theme serving as an accompaniment. This pattern is repeated with the theme descending into the bass, and the two-note "melody" taken up by the treble.

This brief episode comes to a close, and the main theme is heard again in the right hand with a richer accompaniment in the left, then repeated over differing harmonies twice, before another small melody emerges out of the texture of the accompaniment in the left hand. Eventually this melody leads to a restatement of the main theme in both hands (the left hand starting a beat after the right), which introduces a coda-like conclusion to this part of the movement before a series of arpeggios sinks to a growl in the bass.

In effect, what we have just heard is a sort of exposition without a contrasting second theme. The lack of that contrast has made the movement immensely single-minded, with a focus on that opening idea that has made it into an obsessively repeated mantra.

Although this is not a true sonata movement, it does share some of the form's characteristics. The opening section is a sort of exposition, and it is followed by a form of development. The main theme

begins three times in a new key to start this section before it estab-
lishes itself firmly in B-flat minor and cycles through a complete version
of the idea. The theme is played again, with a simple three-note figure
counterpointing the main flow heard first in the bass, then the treble.

Finally, more than one hundred and forty bars into the movement, Beethoven gives us a new musical morsel to chew on, a new
idea. Not much of one, but enough to relieve the overpowering dominance of the main, and up to now sole, theme of the movement. This
second idea is more a rhythm than a melody, but it provides the contrast we need at this point. Based on that drumroll motif back from
the first movement, this "theme" consists of a series of syncopated
notes a half-tone apart, which are eventually repeated in octaves.

Beethoven stays with this idea for a few bars to clear the sound of
the main theme out of our minds, but then plunges back with a fury
into that thematic world. Both hands play the main idea (again the
left hand starts a beat late), starting the pattern a half-tone higher
with each repetition. This sequence leads to a series of repeated notes
in the right hand, which drift higher and higher, eventually being separated from the bass line by four octaves. A series of arpeggios calms
and quiets the texture after this developmental climax, and a snaky
arpeggio descends deep into the bass to set off a series of soft chords
that eventually lead to a restatement of the main theme in its original guise. We have begun the recapitulation.

The main theme at the beginning of the recap is somewhat more
elaborate than at the beginning of the movement, but after that the
recap is modeled very closely on the exposition, in fact more closely

than normal, since the exposition, lacking a second theme, never changed key. Beethoven needs no little tricks in the recap to recast everything in the home key: everything is already there. As in the first movement, Beethoven needs this extreme regularity of form to balance the dynamic passion he has put into the music. A more challenging formal plan would detract from the power of repetition on which Beethoven built this movement.

As the recap approaches the point where the original exposition ended, Beethoven marks an unusual departure. He suggests repeating the development and recapitulation. Exactly why is not clear. We have noted that Beethoven valued forward motion in his works above all else. Repeats became less common as he developed his mature style. To repeat the development at this point of the last movement seems risky, as the mounting drama of the movement could easily be sideswiped by a loss of tension at this point. Many contemporary pianists ignore Beethoven's direction and continue on with the coda. However, Beethoven clearly believed a repeat here was necessary to balance not just this final movement but the proportions of the entire three-movement work. We might quibble with his judgment, but he was seldom wrong in matters of formal design.

So the recapitulation gives way to a repeat of the development, which in turn leads us back into the recap and right to the point to which we had arrived at the end of this section. By now, we have heard that main idea countless times in its various guises and are emotionally exhausted by it.

But Beethoven has one more surprise in store for us. Just as the movement seems to draw to a close, the tempo accelerates and he does the unthinkable. Moments away from the end of this demanding movement and demanding work, he gives us a brand-new theme.

A quick series of chords played in both hands, marked "presto" (very fast), is repeated twice, finally breaking the almost hypnotic effect of that main theme. This totally unexpected bit of music is one of

Beethoven's masterstrokes, musically convincing although formally impossible. It is a perfect example of Beethoven achieving just the right effect by breaking all the rules.

However, this new musical idea disappears as quickly as it came, and the main theme makes one last appearance, spinning through the piano at impossible speeds for a final coda. A frantic descent down the keyboard on an F-minor triad ends the work with three chords deep in the bass. The *Appassionata* has ended exactly where it began.

The *Appassionata* is justly famed as one of Beethoven's major achievements. Its combination of austere musical elements and dynamic passion is hypnotic and deeply original, written in the new musical language Beethoven used for the other masterpieces of his heroic period. It was a language that had taken him fifteen years to develop. Beethoven was at the peak of his compositional powers when he wrote this work, combining passion and technical skill in the manipulation of simple ideas within sonata form. No wonder this music made such an impact on his Viennese audiences, as it does on audiences today. The control Beethoven exercises over his musical material is nearly perfect.

For close to ten years, Beethoven rode the wave of this intense musical tide. However, inevitably, the tide began to recede, marking a new chapter in his life. In this one, at least for a time, personal rather than musical forces were to dominate.

13

Forbidden Love:
The Immortal Beloved

Although no one could have known it at the time, Beethoven's heroic decade reached its climax that cold evening in December of 1808 when he premiered both his Fifth and Sixth Symphonies, his Fourth Piano Concerto and his *Choral Fantasia* for piano and orchestra. It was the success of that extraordinary concert that eventually led to the annuity contract that seemed to secure Beethoven's finances. And reviews of the event, spread throughout Europe, helped create his reputation as the foremost composer of his time. Beethoven in 1809 should have been able to look ahead to a future full of still greater musical achievements.

But they did not materialize. Although he continued to create masterful music, the torrent began to recede. The annuity contract in fact represented the end of a period of extreme creativity, not the beginning. Of Beethoven's great second-period works, only the *Emperor* Concerto, the *Archduke Trio* and the Seventh Symphony were written after the annuity contract was signed. By 1810 and 1811, six months might pass when Beethoven would compose only one or two minor works. Five years earlier, six months was all he had needed to produce three or four masterpieces.

Many things conspired to bring about Beethoven's decline. As noted before, Beethoven was an artist who dreaded repeating himself and who was constantly seeking new artistic problems to solve. The concentrated language of the heroic decade produced many stirring works, but eventually it had to play itself out. There were only so many variations on its themes that Beethoven could write. By early 1810, Beethoven began an experimental phase, in which he was clearly seeking a new direction. For several years he groped slowly and carefully toward this new musical language.

But it was not just within his work that Beethoven's life changed. His external circumstances also took a dramatic turn, as they did for all of Vienna, thanks to Napoleon. Although Austria had been at war with France for the better part of a decade, Vienna itself had been spared the worst effects of the conflict. French troops had briefly occupied the city in 1805 but had left without much incident. Now, in the spring of 1809, the situation was more grave. Napoleon's troops were advancing quickly on the defenseless city. By early May, they had reached its perimeters. The nobility — Beethoven's patrons — fled, and the French swarmed in. The night before the occupation began, the furious French bombardment chased Beethoven to his brother Carl's cellar, pillows stuffed over his ears.

For ten months, until February of 1810, Vienna was an occupied city, submerged in the chaos an occupation brings. Although most of his friends and patrons fled the city for the country, Beethoven remained in Vienna for the duration. It was a devastating period for both the composer and his city. In July of 1809, he wrote to his Berlin publisher, describing the situation:

> You make a great mistake in thinking me so prosperous. [A reference, no doubt, to the just concluded annuity contract.] We have passed through a great deal of misery. When I tell you that since the 4th I have brought into the world little that is connected, only here and there a fragment. The whole

course of events has affected me body and soul; nor can I have the enjoyment of country life, so indispensable to me. . . .
Heaven knows how things will go on; I shall now probably have to change my residence. What a disturbing wild life all around me, nothing but drums, cannon, men, misery of all sorts. . . .

The French left Vienna in early 1810, but the effects of their occupation lingered for years. Under the weight of war debt, Austria collapsed financially and in 1811 devalued its currency by 80 percent. Suddenly, financial concerns again became a constant worry for Beethoven. Since his annuity contract had been expressed in 1809 currency, the effect of the devaluation was to reduce his annual income from 4,000 florins (a generous sum) to 800 florins (a useless one). Beethoven spent several years trying to have the original amount restored, eventually suing his three benefactors.

But more than the war affected Beethoven's peace of mind. His personal worries, held at bay for a decade by his near-total concentration on his art, were ready to attack anew. To be sure, Beethoven's physical and mental health had been gradually deteriorating during the heroic years, yet the all-consuming effort of his work had seemed to carry him beyond the harm of these troubling forces. But now, with his musical inspiration fading, Beethoven could no longer ignore his personal demons. Out of the growing darkness they reared up to confront him. Concerns about his health, his finances and his future began to obsess him. More and more, to counteract these anxieties, Beethoven turned his thoughts to the potential salvation of love, marriage and domestic stability.

Beethoven had always been ambivalent about family life. His own had been torturous and difficult, and he had acquired all the habits of a perennial bachelor. Nonetheless, the next ten years of his life were to be dominated by a yearning for home and family, a desire that was tragically disappointed time and again.

The first recorded hint of that desire is a sudden increase in the number of women in Beethoven's life around 1810. Between 1800 and 1809, only two names have been linked romantically with Beethoven: Giulietta Guicciardi and Josephine Deym. In the following two years, we hear of Therese Malfatti, the dedicatee of *Für Elise*, Bettina Brentano, whom Beethoven met in the summer of 1810, Marie Bigot, whom he knew in the fall of that year, and Amalie Sebald, who met the composer the following summer. Beethoven's relationship with each of these women was different. He seems to have formed a relatively harmless infatuation with the young Amalie Sebald, and probably paid a little too much flirtatious attention to the married Marie Bigot. With Bettina Brentano, the situation was more serious. Bettina was one of the most interesting young women of her time, friendly (if not intimately involved) with Goethe and a number of other German intellectuals and artists. Through Bettina, Beethoven struck up a relationship and eventually met Goethe at the summer resort of Teplitz. Bettina both flattered Beethoven with her unabashed hero worship and probably attracted him as well by her open innocence.

But it was with Therese Malfatti that Beethoven developed his most serious relationship, in the spring of 1810. Although details are vague, it seems he proposed to Therese, who was the daughter of one of his doctors. We know this only because the composer wrote a hurried letter to his friend Franz Wegeler in Bonn asking him to track down his birth certificate. Exactly what happened is a mystery, although the engagement was certainly broken off. Musical lore has it that the Malfatti family refused to have Beethoven as a son-in-law.

Finally, probably in 1812, Beethoven formed the relationship he had been seeking all his life, falling desperately in love with a woman who tragically was not free to fully reciprocate his affection. The identity of this woman remains unknown to this day, but the affair inspired one of the most devastating chapters in Beethoven's life.

We know of the relationship because of a single letter Beethoven wrote to his love, found among his papers after his death. The letter was undated but is now generally believed to have been written in the summer of 1812. We don't know if it was ever sent. Even if he had not sealed the importance of this letter by keeping it for fifteen years, its significance for him and his life would be obvious from a single reading. This is the famous letter to his "Immortal Beloved":

July 6, in the morning
My angel, my all, my very self — Only a few words today
and at that with pencil (with yours) — Not until tomorrow
will my lodgings be definitely determined upon — what a
useless waste of time — Why this deep sorrow when necessity speaks? Can our love endure except through sacrifices,
through not demanding everything from one another; can
you change the fact that you are not wholly mine, I not
wholly thine — Oh God, look out into the beauties of
nature and comfort yourself with that which must be —
Love demands everything and that very justly — thus it is to
me with you, and to you with me. If only you do not forget
that I must live for me and for you; if we were wholly united
you would feel the pain of it as little as I — My journey was
a fearful one; I did not reach here until 4 o'clock yesterday
morning. Lacking horses the post-coach chose another route,
but what an awful one; at the stage before the last I was
warned not to travel at night; I was made fearful of a forest,
but that only made me the more eager — and I was wrong.
The coach must needs break down on the wretched road, a
bottomless mud road. Without such postilions as I had with
me I should have remained stuck in the road. Esterhazy,
traveling the usual road here, had the same fate with eight
horses that I had with four. — Yet, I got some pleasure out of

it, as I always do when I successfully overcome difficulties —
Now a quick change to things internal from things eternal.
We shall surely see each other soon; moreover, today I cannot share with you the thoughts I have had during the last
few days touching my own life — If our hearts were always
close together, I would have none of these. My heart is full
of so many things to say to you — ah — there are moments
when I feel that speech amounts to nothing at all — Cheer
up — remain my true, my only love, my all as I am yours.
The gods must send us the rest, what for us must and shall
be —

Your faithful Ludwig

Evening, Monday, July 6

You are suffering, my dearest creature — Just now have I
learned that letters must be posted very early in the morning
on Mondays — or on Thursdays — the only days on which
the mail-coach goes from here to K. — You are suffering —
Ah, wherever I am, there you are also — I will arrange it
with you and me that I can live with you. What a life!!!!!
thus!!!! without you — pursued by the goodness of mankind
hither and thither — which I as little want to deserve as I
deserve it — Humility of man toward man — it pains me —
and when I consider myself in relation to the universe, what
am I and what is he — whom we call the greatest — and yet
— herein lies the divine in man — I weep when I reflect
that you will probably not receive the first report from me
until Saturday — Much as you love me — I love you more —
But do not ever conceal yourself from me — good night —
As I am taking the baths I must go to bed — Oh God — so
near! so far! Is not our love truly a heavenly structure, and
also as firm as the vault of Heaven? —

Good morning, on July 7

Though still in bed, my thoughts go out to you, my Immortal Beloved, now and then joyfully, then sadly, waiting to learn whether or not fate will hear us — I can only live wholly with you or not at all — Yes, I am resolved to wander so long away from you until I can fly to your arms and say that I am really at home with you, and can send my soul enwrapped in you into the land of spirits — Yes, unhappily, it must be so — You will be the more contained since you know my fidelity to you. No one else can ever possess my heart — never — never — Oh God, why must one be parted from one whom one so loves. And yet my life in Vienna is now a wretched life — Your love makes me at once the happiest and unhappiest of men — At my age I need a steady, quiet life — can that be so in our connection? My angel, I have just been told that the mail-coach goes every day — and I must close at once so that you may receive the letter at once. — Be calm, only by a calm consideration of our existence can we achieve our purpose to live together — Be calm — love me — today — yesterday — what tearful longings for you — you — you — my life — my all — farewell — Oh continue to love me — never misjudge the most faithful heart of your beloved.

ever thine

ever mine

ever ours   L.

Never before had Beethoven expressed himself with such passion to a lover, and even for a man given to extravagant outbursts, this letter is unparalleled in his correspondence. Beethoven is transparent in his feelings as he struggles with his love for this unattainable woman. The emotional tone changes from line to line, but it is interesting to note that by the letter's third section, the one written on the morning of July 7, Beethoven is already backing away from the commitment his love presses on him. At one and the same time, he is transfixed by the deep feeling he has for this woman, but resists it as well.

Needless to say, the discovery of the letter led to immediate speculation about the identity of its intended recipient. As the date included only a day and month, the letter has inspired a cornucopia of interpretations. More effort in Beethoven studies has been expended on unmasking this mystery woman than on any other single subject. For 150 years, various biographers made a case for just about every woman Beethoven had ever known — from Anton Schindler's nomination of Giulietta Guicciardi to Alexander Thayer's of Therese von Brunsvik, to San Galli's of Amalie Sebald. Then, in 1977, the American scholar Maynard Solomon went back to the clues liberally distributed throughout the letter and argued convincingly that the Immortal Beloved was Antonie Brentano, Bettina's sister-in-law, whom Beethoven had known for several years before the events described in the letter occurred.

If Solomon is right, the pain of this affair would have been doubly difficult for the composer. Antonie and Franz Brentano were Beethoven's friends; both before and after the summer of 1812 he relied on their hospitality and generosity. Under no circumstances would he have attempted to destroy what he believed to be the sanctity of their life together. Toni Brentano seems to have been a sensitive woman prone to illness. As mentioned earlier, Beethoven is known to have visited her home on several occasions to ease her melancholy by simply improvising on the piano without speaking a word. Whether or not she was the Immortal Beloved, she and Beethoven had a stronger than usual friendship. She seems to have been one of the few to be able to pierce through the thick shell that deafness, loneliness, eccentricity and unhappiness had enclosed around him. In a letter in 1819, she referred to Beethoven as "this great, excellent person" who "is as a human being greater than as an artist." There have been very few, either during Beethoven's lifetime or since, who could say such a thing about him with conviction. A deep affection speaks in those simple words.

Maybe it was not Toni Brentano to whom Beethoven wrote his passionate letter of Monday, July 6. Perhaps it was one of the many other candidates who have been brought forward over the years. Or maybe it was a woman about whom we know nothing and whose name has never been linked to Beethoven's. In the end, it doesn't really matter. What is important is that the letter to the Immortal Beloved represents as decisive a turning point in Beethoven's life as the crisis in Heiligenstadt had a decade earlier. The attachment to the Immortal Beloved seems to have been the last of its kind Beethoven ever formed. With the death of this love, all love — at least, all romantic love — seems to have perished for him as well. Along with it perished all thoughts of marriage. After 1812, Beethoven never mentions it again. The significance of the relationship for Beethoven is not that he fell so completely in love (he had done that before) but that the failure of this affair seems to have broken his spirit.

Clues to this breakdown are not confined to the love letter itself. Beethoven began keeping a sort of diary just a few months after he wrote the famous letter, in September of 1812. Its first two entries appear to refer pathetically to the ruined affair:

Submission, absolute submission to your fate, only this can give you the sacrifice . . . to the servitude — Oh, hard struggle! — Turn everything which remains to be done to planning the long journey — you must yourself find all that your most blessed wish can offer, you must force it to your will — keep always of the same mind. . . .

Thou mayest no longer be a man, not for thyself, only for others, for thee there is no longer happiness except in thyself, in thy art — O God, give me strength to conquer myself, nothing

~~must chain me to life. Thus everything connected to A. will go~~
to destruction.

To forgo a great act which might have been and remains
so — Oh what a difference compared with an unstudied
life which often rose in my fancy — Oh fearful conditions
which do not suppress my feeling for domesticity, but whose
execution, O God, God, look down upon the unhappy B.,
do not permit it to last thus much longer —

Beethoven was still feeling the effects of the affair in the early
months of 1813, when he seems to have reached his lowest ebb. In the
summer of that year, there is at least one report that he attempted suicide by starvation. Friends found him "in a deplorable state," dirty and
disheveled, even more careless of his physical appearance than usual.
Most significantly, he had almost completely stopped composing.
Beethoven had managed to create two important works in 1811 and
1812 — his Seventh and Eighth Symphonies — but in 1813 there was
a virtual compositional drought. A man for whom composing had
been as natural and necessary as breathing just stopped writing. This
factor more than any other reveals the depths of Beethoven's distress.
Where the Heiligenstadt crisis of 1802 had served to liberate his creative energy, the failure of the affair with the Immortal Beloved seems
to have had the opposite effect. And without his work to sustain him,
the increasing weight of his day-to-day problems threatened to over-
whelm him.

A temporary deliverance came in the spring of 1813, in the form
of an unlikely offer by one of Vienna's more bizarre characters, Johann
Nepomuk Maelzel. We know Maelzel today as the inventor of the
metronome, but in the first decades of the nineteenth century, he daz-
zled Vienna as an inventor and would-be composer — part entrepre-
neur, part showman, part charlatan.

Maelzel and Beethoven joined forces as a result of the inventor's fascination with clockwork mechanical instruments. One of his most successful devices had been an artificial trumpeter that could play real music. In the fall of 1812, Maelzel was working on his crowning achievement, the Panharmonicon — a complete mechanical orchestra, capable of playing a full symphonic work. Maelzel was determined to show it off to best advantage, so he approached Vienna's greatest composer, Beethoven, to write a showpiece for his overgrown music box. Such a request was not quite as outrageous as it may seem. In the last years of his life, Mozart had composed a few pieces for similar contraptions. For whatever reason, Beethoven agreed to Maelzel's request.

Maelzel planned to take the Panharmonicon to England, where he expected to make a fortune demonstrating it. So when the English general Wellington won a decisive victory over Napoleon in June 1813, in the Spanish town of Vittoria, Maelzel and Beethoven decided to commemorate the battle in the composition for the Panharmonicon. Full of sound and fury and bugle flourishes, the work was originally called the *Battle Symphony* and later, *Wellington's Victory*.

It may seem implausible that the composer of the *Appassionata* and the Fifth Symphony would bother with such a potboiler (and the *Battle Symphony* is arguably the worst piece of music Beethoven ever wrote), but even more implausible is that it was this work of all others that made him a superstar. With the *Battle Symphony*, Beethoven vaulted into the circle of fame reserved not just for well-known composers but for true public celebrities. With it, all Europe now knew his name, connoisseurs and the general public alike.

Eventually Maelzel gave up on the Panharmonicon and simply presented the *Battle Symphony* as a showpiece for conventional orchestra. For two special charity concerts he had arranged for December of 1813, Maelzel premiered the *Battle Symphony* along with Beethoven's Seventh to create what were perhaps the composer's two most successful nights in the concert hall. The concerts' charitable purpose persuaded all Vienna's most famous musicians to play in the orchestra. Louis Spohr was among the first violins, Gustave Meyerbeer among the seconds, and Antonio Salieri, at sixty-three still very much a feature of Viennese musical life, played the bass drum.

"Applause rose to the point of ecstasy," wrote one reviewer of the first concert. The second movement of the Seventh Symphony was immediately encored during each concert, and the *Battle Symphony* was an unbelievable success. Although some in Vienna (and many since) despaired that the sublime Beethoven had stooped to the creation of such a work, Anton Schindler, Beethoven's amanuensis and first biographer, probably was right when he wrote: "A work like the battle-symphony had to come in order that divergent opinions might be united and the mouths of all opponents, of whatever kind, silenced." The night of the first concert, according to Schindler, was "one of the most important moments in the life of the master, at which all the hitherto divergent voices . . . united in proclaiming him worthy of the laurel." By dropping his forbidding countenance just for a second, and by letting the general public know he was willing to write them music they could understand and enjoy without the slightest furrowed brow, Beethoven liberated the pent-up adulation Vienna wanted to bestow upon him. Vienna knew he was a great and famous musician but had still found his music difficult, intellectual and forbidding. Now they could say with sincerity that they too, not just the elite, enjoyed the music of the great master.

Due to the success of the *Battle Symphony*, Beethoven's fame leapt to new heights the following year, 1814, perhaps the most publicly successful twelve months of his life. Suddenly, his music, which had fallen into something of a popular decline, was magically restored to Vienna concert halls. Beethoven was everywhere. His symphonies were featured in concerts, his string quartets graced every aristocratic salon. Even *Fidelio*, which had been unenthusiastically received twice before, was hauled out of mothballs, given a thorough revision and presented again, this time to overwhelming success. Beethoven enjoyed a public acclaim he had never before experienced.

The summit of Beethoven's celebrity came between September of 1814 and June of 1815 during the Congress of Vienna, a ten-month-long peace conference that redrew the political map of Europe. Napoleon had been defeated at Waterloo and was in exile, and the nobility of Europe descended on the Austrian capital to divide the spoils of victory. For months, kings, princes, czars and assorted nobles bargained during the day and entertained themselves at night. Hundreds of concerts were given, with Beethoven and his music front and center at many of them. The new and improved *Fidelio* was one of the first works to be presented to the assembled monarchs; the *Battle Symphony* and the Seventh were performed to delirious acclaim. Beethoven was feted by royalty, his presence hotly demanded by competing rulers eager to display their appreciation of Europe's reigning musical genius. The turnaround in Beethoven's fortunes was remarkable. In the summer of 1813, he may have attempted suicide. Two summers later, he was the most honored artist in Europe.

Beethoven was deeply gratified by the extraordinary attention he received during the months of the Congress. A decade later, he could not remember those days without great emotion. However, the honors that fate had finally bestowed could not entirely erase Beethoven's inner turmoil. His latest compositions were still few in number and mainly uninspiring: during the Congress period, he produced some of his least interesting works. After the shouting had died down, and the monarchs of Europe had returned home, Beethoven was left with a legacy of loneliness that the events of 1814 and 1815 had masked but not erased. The loss of the Immortal Beloved had created a void in his heart, one he spent the next five bitter years attempting to fill.

14

Expropriated Love: Karl

Europe in 1815 was a far different place from the revolutionary continent that had formed the backdrop of Beethoven's youth and early manhood. Twenty years of war had shattered the Enlightenment ideals that had inspired the best minds of the late eighteenth century and which had been the source of Beethoven's own personal philosophy. In 1815, who could heroize Napoleon, a man who had turned liberty, equality and fraternity into conquest, empire and privilege? Who anymore could celebrate reason and human enlightenment, surrounded by the detritus of war? Europe was exhausted and had lost its political nerve. So many of the monarchs Napoleon had deposed — supposedly forever — were once again seated on their countries' thrones. Reactionism was the new reality.

However, two decades of revolutionary sentiment could not be entirely erased from the minds and hearts of Europe's people. The monarchs of old may have reappeared, but the countries they governed were new. The feudal privilege of divine right, which still held some sway as late as the eighteenth century, was a dead principle by the nineteenth. Kings and czars now depended on secret police and repressive measures, rather than on ancient authority, for their power. Austria, especially, under its chancellor, Metternich, became a virtual police state. Its citizens, frightened of the police and weary of politics, embraced a new life-style, abandoning themselves to frenzied pleasures and desperate joys. It was a time not unlike the Roaring Twenties, a hundred years later.

Beethoven had little sympathy for either the politics or the society of the new age. Although the Napoleonic wars had shaken his beliefs, they had not toppled them. He was still a man of the Enlightenment, a defender of freedom and liberty. His outspoken denunciation of the abuses he saw in Vienna after 1815 would have landed him in prison had his fame not protected him. And Beethoven cared little for the mad pursuit of pleasure that swept over the city he had called home for twenty years. His kind of serious music was being abandoned, he feared, in favor of a new lighter, happier form of expression. The operas of Rossini were Vienna's current musical rage. Within the space of a few years, Beethoven had passed from flaming musical revolutionary to still-famous but fading anachronism.

Meanwhile, Beethoven's personal woes continued unabated. His hearing deteriorated severely in 1813 and 1814, causing him both professional and personal problems. His last public performance as a pianist took place during these years. Louis Spohr, later a celebrated composer, painted this pathetic portrait of a rehearsal of the *Archduke* Trio in which Beethoven participated in the spring of 1814:

It was not a treat, for, in the first place, the piano was badly out of tune, which Beethoven minded little, since he did not hear it; and secondly, on account of his deafness there was scarcely anything left of the virtuosity of the artist which had formerly been so greatly admired. In forte passages the poor deaf man pounded on the keys till the strings jangled, and in piano he played so softly that whole groups of tones were omitted, so that the music was unintelligible unless one could look into the pianoforte part. I was deeply saddened at so hard a fate. If it is a great misfortune for any one to be deaf, how shall a musician endure it without giving way to despair? Beethoven's continual melancholy was no longer a riddle to me.

Spohr didn't know, of course, the deeper causes of Beethoven's unhappiness — his unhappy love affair and flagging musical inspiration. Beethoven's deafness merely increased his isolation and need for some form of emotional solace. But following the loss of the Immortal Beloved, he was not likely to seek romantic love to ease his pain. Something or someone else must take its place.

And someone else did: his nephew Karl. In November of 1815, Beethoven's brother, Carl, died, setting in motion one of the most tempestuous chapters in the composer's life. For several years, Beethoven's musical activity virtually ceased as he focused his entire being on an obsession that shadowed the rest of his life.

Karl van Beethoven was nine years old when his father's death propelled him into the center of Beethoven's emotional life. Carl had always wanted his brother to help his wife, Johanna, raise his son after his death, and two years earlier had asked Beethoven to consider this role. Little did Carl suspect that this simple request would plunge the family into a fierce battle that was dragged through the courts of Vienna for half a decade.

Carl van Beethoven and Johanna Reiss had been married in 1806, just a few months before Karl was born. For some reason, Beethoven seems to have hated his sister-in-law from the moment she entered his family's life. Perhaps it was because she was a woman far removed from the aristocratic ideal of femininity he admired. Her relationship with Carl was stormy and often violent. Carl was said to have beaten Johanna regularly and once stabbed her through the hand with a table knife. In 1811, he had her arrested for stealing money from him, and she was convicted of theft. Beethoven had nothing but scorn for her.

Carl's will originally appointed Johanna and Beethoven co-guardians of Karl. However, before Carl died, Beethoven had him amend the will so that he alone would exercise guardianship. Carl seems to have done so without protest. Beethoven later explained why he demanded the changes. "I came upon the will by chance," he wrote. "If what I had seen was really to be the original text, then passages had to be stricken out. This I had my brother bring about since I did not wish to be bound up in this with such a bad woman in a matter of such importance as the education of the child."

On his deathbed, Carl finally recognized Beethoven's true motive: he wanted to take sole charge of Karl, denying Johanna any contact with her own son. Alarmed, Carl hastily dictated a codicil to the will the day before he died:

> Having learned that my brother, Hr. Ludwig van Beethoven, desires after my death to take wholly to himself my son Karl, and wholly to withdraw him from the supervision and training of his mother, and inasmuch as the best of harmony does not exist between my brother and my wife, I have found it necessary to add to my will that I by no means desire that my son be taken away from his mother, but that he shall always and so long as his future career permits remain with his mother, to which end the guardianship of him is to be exercised by her as well as my brother. Only by unity can the object which I had in view in appointing my brother guardian of my son be attained; wherefore, for the welfare of my child, I recommend compliance to my wife and more moderation to my brother.
>
> God permit them to be harmonious for the sake of my child's welfare. This is the last wish of the dying husband and brother.

Carl's last wish was not to be heeded by either wife or brother. For five years, they fought each other in the streets and in the courts of Vienna for custody of the boy. The moderation Carl had recommended to his brother was ignored, being replaced by an obsessive pursuit of Karl and hatred of Johanna. Denied a natural family of his own, Beethoven seemed determined to appropriate the next best thing to it. He pursued Karl with a ferocity that was not relaxed even when it was obviously harmful to the boy and to himself. No amount of counsel, friendly or otherwise, could dissuade Beethoven from this quest.

Beethoven began his campaign for the boy instantly upon his brother's death. Despite the clear intent of the codicil of Carl's will, Beethoven petitioned the Viennese courts to overturn the decision to appoint Johanna Karl's co-guardian. He claimed that Johanna was unfit as a mother on the basis of the questionable embezzlement charge brought against her four years earlier. After two further petitions made within weeks, Beethoven won his case. Karl, at ten, was removed from his mother and his home by court order in February of 1816 and placed in a private school, run by Cajetan Giannatasio del Rio, a well-known Viennese educator. Aghast at the loss of her son, Johanna repeatedly went to the school to try to take Karl home, at least on one occasion disguised as a man. Beethoven then sought and won a further court order preventing Johanna from having any contact with Karl unless Beethoven or his representative was present.

His victory over Johanna seemed complete, and his joy was profound. That it came at the expense of a mother and son denied all contact with each other occasionally gave Beethoven pause, but never enough to make him change course. Beethoven never wavered in his belief that he was doing the right thing for Karl. And he loved the boy, but with a love fed by extremes.

Beethoven's behavior toward his nephew veered from overpowering affection to undisciplined rage. Karl could never depend on his uncle's moods, nor predict them. In Karl was wrapped up so much of Beethoven's longing for family that he started to believe that the boy was his real son. In May of 1816, Beethoven wrote to Ferdinand Ries:

"You know that in some regard I am now father to the lovely lad you saw me with. . . . Hardly can I live alone three months on my annual salary . . . and now the additional burden of maintaining a poor orphan." Despite the obvious evidence to the contrary, Beethoven created a new status for Karl. First he made him into an orphan; later, into his natural son.

Beethoven's relationship with Johanna was even more confused and contradictory. Although he never ceased expressing his contempt for her in the strongest terms, Johanna herself believed that Beethoven was in love with her. She may well have been right. His exaggerated hatred of her seems to have been matched by a furtive attention that was almost surely sexual. Beethoven loved to hear and retell stories of Johanna's supposed licentiousness: that she was a prostitute, that she had danced naked at a ball. Every so often during the custody battle, he would relax his opposition to her and become extremely friendly, only to regret his behavior soon after and redouble his cruelty. His frankly irrational attitudes toward this woman suggest a deeply divided nature. On the one hand, she was the mother of the boy he was treating as his son, and what could be more natural than to have "father" and mother united? Yet Beethoven's fear of Johanna's influence over Karl, and perhaps over himself, led him to attempt to erase all traces of her existence in the boy's life. To have Karl to himself, Johanna had to be figuratively and symbolically murdered. No wonder that this episode in Beethoven's life has intrigued more than one psychoanalyst in this century.

For the first year of the guardianship, Karl attended a private boarding school in Vienna. While Karl was there, relations between Beethoven and Johanna, while far from calm, were at least contained. Johanna tried to see Karl as often as she could; Beethoven did everything in his power to prevent these meetings. Through 1816 and 1817, an uneasy truce settled over the two combatants, and Beethoven's creative forces, so long stilled, began tentatively to reemerge. At the beginning of 1818, however, Beethoven made a fatal mistake: he decided to remove Karl from his school and bring him home to live. The move was a disaster. Beethoven was a deaf, eccentric, forty-eight-year-old bachelor whose only experience of family life — his own — had been dismal. He had few models, if any, on which to base paternal behavior. His treatment of Karl was inconsistent, emotional and irrational. Beethoven's most important biographer, Alexander Thayer, writes:

> In all his life he had never had an occasion to give a thought to the duties which such an office [fatherhood] involved. In the conduct of his own affairs he had always permitted himself to be swayed by momentary impulses, emotion and sometimes violent passions, and could not suddenly develop the habits of calm reflection, unimpassioned judgement and consistent behaviour essential to the training of a careless and wayward boy. In his treatment of him he flew from one extreme to the other — from almost cruel severity to almost limitless indulgence, and, for this reason, failed to inspire either respect for his authority or deep affection for his person.

Under Beethoven's sole supervision, Karl was tossed about on the seas of his guardian's emotional instability. Finally, he could take it no longer. In the fall of 1818, he escaped to his mother's house, bringing harrowing tales about Beethoven's treatment of him and of his constant demand that Karl repudiate Johanna. Alarmed and emboldened by her son's distress, Johanna decided to take the case back to court, which she did in December of 1818. The uneasy peace between Johanna and Beethoven was shattered.

There were two court systems in Vienna, one for the nobility and one for everyone else. The van Beethoven case had been heard in the nobles' court, the Landrecht, under the mistaken belief, common in Vienna, that the Beethovens were of aristocratic ancestry. (Even today, people often confuse the common Flemish *van* with the aristocratic German *von*.) In the middle of this second hearing, the Landrecht discovered almost by accident that the Beethovens had no claim to nobility and that therefore the court had no jurisdiction in the case. It referred the matter to the common court system, the Vienna Magistracy.

This change of venue was calamitous for Beethoven on two counts. It seems clear that Beethoven had used his patrons to influence the Landrecht on his behalf in the original deliberations. In the common court system, such influence would be of less, if any, significance. From the beginning, the Magistracy took a dim view of Beethoven's arguments and position.

But even more devastating was the blow to Beethoven's sense of himself, to be declared publicly and unequivocally a commoner. While he had never consciously lied about his background, neither had he scotched rumors of his noble ancestry. Beethoven believed that he belonged to a "natural" aristocracy, one conferred by talent and genius, and that this circumstance had somehow transformed the mundane facts of his birth and upbringing. The public repudiation of this notion hurt him deeply. As he put it himself: "It is singular, as far as I know, that there is a hiatus here which ought to be filled, for my nature shows that I do not belong among this plebeian mass. The common citizen should be excluded from higher men, and I have gotten amongst them."

The proceedings in the Magistracy began in January of 1819 and lasted the better part of a year. Unlike the Landrecht, this court was immediately more sympathetic to Johanna, and Beethoven began a series of maneuvers to prevent a decision being brought against him. He sent Karl to another private school, made plans to appoint a delegate to exercise the day-to-day responsibilities of the guardianship, considered a scheme to send Karl out of the country. All were to no avail. In October of 1819, the court removed Karl from Beethoven's sole guardianship and returned him to the custody of his mother.

Beethoven's first reaction to this setback was to plan to kidnap Karl and flee Austria, but wiser counsel prevailed. Instead, he launched an immediate appeal of the Magistracy's decision, dredging up the old charges of Johanna's immorality, which had weighed so heavily against her in the original hearing. Again Beethoven attempted to curry favor with the aristocratic judges of the appeals court. This time the stratagems worked. Johanna's victory turned out to be quite short-lived. In early 1820, the appeals court reversed the Magistracy's decision and returned Karl to Beethoven. Johanna made a desperate appeal to the emperor himself, which proved unsuccessful. In July of 1820, Karl was given to Beethoven once and for all and remained his ward until the composer's death almost seven years later.

Karl van Beethoven had been nine years old when the custody suit began and was fourteen when it ended. These five years had been almost unceasingly traumatic for him. Not only had he been unnaturally torn from his mother just weeks after his father's death but he had been used as a token for years in the battle between his mother and his uncle. Johanna seems to have been less guilty than Beethoven, but each adult filled Karl's head with poison about the other. No wonder that Karl's teachers and other guardians noticed signs of delinquency and suspiciousness in his character.

Beethoven's relations with Karl, though not completely resolved by the final court decision in 1820, were eased, and the interminable legal battle, which had caused him so much anxiety and virtually stilled his pen, was over. Toward Johanna, Beethoven attempted to be the graceful victor, holding out an olive branch of reconciliation more than once, but his own conflicting attitudes toward her prevented him from establishing any consistent relationship.

Beethoven had played out some tremendous internal battles in the years of the fight over Karl's future. Deep-seated conflicts con-

15

Beyond Love:
The Final Years

The long custody suit had for a time virtually halted Beethoven's creative life. By 1818, many of his closest friends and acquaintances felt that he was written out, artistically and emotionally exhausted. He had not composed a work of real substance since his Eighth Symphony in 1812, six years earlier. His physical health was rapidly deteriorating and his mental health was, if anything, worse. Beethoven seemed a man for whom renewed creative work was impossible.

By this time, as well, Beethoven had to confront a major shift in musical style away from the intellectually precise, reasoned forms of writing on which he completely depended. The Enlightenment models — especially sonata form — were giving way to smaller forms of organization, based on the song and imbued with a tunefulness that taxed no one's intellectual faculties. The age of Mozart, Haydn and Beethoven was becoming the age of Schubert, Weber and Rossini.

"You will hear nothing of me here," grumbled Beethoven to a friend visiting Vienna in the summer of 1822. "What should you hear? *Fidelio*? They cannot give it, nor do they want to listen to it. The symphonies? They have no time for them. My concertos? Everyone grinds out only the stuff he himself has made. The solo pieces? They went out of fashion here long ago, and here fashion is everything. At the most, Schuppanzigh occasionally digs up a quartet. . . ."

Ironically, Beethoven's dilemma was heightened by the knowledge that it was largely his own work that had laid the foundation for the new musical styles. The very emotion that Beethoven packed into such works as the Fifth and Seventh Symphonies seemed to render traditional sonata form irrelevant. Beethoven had liberated emotion from formal constraints in music. In abandoning these constraints, the younger generation was only following a trail he himself had blazed, or so they thought.

However, Beethoven could not follow that path himself. He could not, or would not, give up the musical principles on which he had been raised, chiefly the logic of sonata form. But Beethoven did know that renovation was needed. The heroic style of the century's first decade had run its course; this he more or less proved to himself when he unsuccessfully attempted to revive it during the Vienna Congress years. For several years, Beethoven wrote as though he could not see a way out of his predicament. The few pieces he composed during his years of relative silence are curious and not entirely successful attempts to create a new, more lyrical, musical language.

Then the miraculous happened. Beethoven started to compose once again in earnest. He began tentatively in 1817, in the middle of the custody battle, and then more confidently in 1819 and 1820 as the suit drew to a close. Over the next seven years, he produced a body of music — the late works — that some feel is his greatest achievement. Controversial when they appeared and controversial ever since, the late works remain one of the mysteries of classical music. To this day, they fit uneasily into our scheme of musical history and continuity.

The Beethoven who emerged phoenix-like from his trials was, in these works, both more heroic and more personal than ever before. Although consistent with Beethoven's compositional past, these works are nonetheless strikingly fresh and original. Gone is the powerful logical control that seems to dominate every note of Beethoven's middle-period works. At the same time gargantuan and intimate, the late works sound like a kind of interior monologue, a musing on art and life, even when they take place on the scale of the Ninth Symphony or the *Hammerklavier* Sonata. These are works we overhear as much as hear.

For a new listener, and in fact for many seasoned listeners, the late works can be something of a challenge. Even professional musicians find them heavy going, best appreciated after the music of Beethoven's two previous periods has become familiar. On the other hand, the late works are so original that even a slight exposure to them will broaden your notion of what music can achieve.

The late works fall into two separate categories, the monumental and the intensely personal. The first group may have been inspired by an offer Beethoven received in the 1820s. A publisher suggested bringing out an edition of his complete works, with Beethoven providing one last example in each of the forms in which he had worked: symphony, concerto, sonata and so on. Although the project fell through, the valedictory idea appealed to the composer. As he surveyed a changing world with which he had increasingly little connection, Beethoven felt a need to set his final stamp on the forms he had worked with all his life.

Consequently, he set out (consciously or not) to write a definitive work in each form — the piano sonata to end all piano sonatas, the symphony to end all symphonies. The result was the *Hammerklavier* Piano Sonata, the op. 130 string quartet, the *Diabelli* Piano Variations, the *Missa Solemnis* and finally the Ninth Symphony. Each one of these works is not only massive in size and architecture, extending the concept of form beyond all previous boundaries, but is also suffused with an intensity previously unknown in music history. Even Beethoven had never before so openly expressed his inner thoughts and feelings in works of art.

The intimacy that characterizes even the most monumental of these works was given special prominence in the second category of Beethoven's late works, his very last piano sonatas and string quartets. These works are almost painful to listen to at times because of their depth and emotional transparency. Normally, we expect a work of art to have a certain amount of spectacle built into it. Even the most moving pieces — of theater or music — exist at a certain distance from us, built for our observation. We can protect ourselves as viewers and listeners from being distressed by these works with the knowledge that they are products of an artist, and depict imaginary, not real, situations. Even works as involving as the *Eroica* Symphony and the *Appassionata* Sonata are clearly display pieces, canvases on which musical emotions are projected.

However, in the late works, Beethoven drops the techniques of display and writes music so disarming and unpredictable that we feel we are coming into direct contact with the composer's very personality and soul. The experience can be a bit unnerving as well as exhilarating. The late works force us to listen to music in new ways that push us past the ordinary into the otherworldly.

That this highly spiritual, almost religious music could come from a man who had just spent five years engaged in an obsessive custody battle remains a complex puzzle. The composer celebrating universal brotherhood in the Ninth Symphony's "Ode to Joy" is far removed from the tormented man scheming to deny his sister-in-law her child. The artist and the man seem to exist on two different planes, as though Beethoven had retreated into a perfect world of his own making when he picked up his pen. The outside world became a separate place, to be tolerated only as long as necessary.

Perhaps Beethoven's deep spiritual focus in his late music was the result of his almost total isolation from society. His deafness was now complete, although he conversed with many associates using his ever-present Conversation Books. He became a notorious figure in Vienna, traipsing through the streets in rain or shine, singing, humming, howling to himself, occasionally noting down an idea in a small notebook. Young boys would follow him for sport. One summer he was mistaken for a tramp and arrested by an overzealous police officer, who reported to his superior that the vagrant "continually claimed he was the composer, Beethoven." Virtually everyone who came into contact with Beethoven during these years was struck by the pitiable state to which he was reduced, the great genius of music who could not strike a simple chord on the piano and be sure he was not creating a horrible dissonance.

Although isolated by his deafness, Beethoven was never a recluse. He continued to communicate with a number of associates and friends, albeit with difficulty, about plans for new works and performances of old ones, about politics, art, religion and just plain gossip. He also carried on a constant correspondence with publishers. However, indecision and anxiety constantly plagued him. A projected trip to London, which might have been a great success, was planned three times yet eventually abandoned. Worried about money, Beethoven entered into simultaneous negotiations with several publishers for his *Missa Solemnis*, alienating them all. Even the simplest business arrangements became hopelessly complex and drawn out.

The truest "events" of Beethoven's last years are his compositions, each of which caused him immense effort and struggle. Gone was the composer who could work on three or four compositions at the same time. Beethoven was now working on a different scale. "You see, for some time past I find I no longer settle down to write so easily," Beethoven confided to a friend in 1822. "I sit and think and think and what I have to say is all there, but it will not get down to paper. I dread beginning works. . . . Once I have begun, then all goes well."

Beethoven labored long and hard over the compositions of his final period. The *Hammerklavier* Sonata, op. 106, was begun in the fall of 1817; it wasn't completed until 1819. His final three piano sonatas, op. 109, 110 and 111, occupied the better part of 1820 and 1821. The *Missa Solemnis*, a Mass begun in 1819 for Archduke Rudolph's installation as Bishop of Olmutz in March of 1820, wasn't completed until 1822. The Ninth Symphony, begun in 1817 and then abandoned, was taken up again in 1823 and finished the following year. The last five string quartets were written from late 1824 to late 1826.

The immense effort required by these works was due partly to Beethoven's age (he was now in his mid-fifties) and deteriorating health (he suffered from severe rheumatic fever and jaundice by this time), but primarily to the kind of music he was now writing. Beethoven was working on a massive scale, entering uncharted modes of form and expression. All of this took time and tremendous powers of concentration, as Anton Schindler discovered one summer's day in 1822, when he visited the composer at work on his Mass:

I arrived at the master's house in Modling. It was four o'clock in the afternoon. As soon as we entered we learned that in the morning both servants had gone away, and that there had been a quarrel after midnight which had disturbed all the neighbors, because as a consequence of a long vigil both had gone to sleep and the food which had been prepared had become unpalatable. In the living room, behind a locked door, we heard the master singing parts of the fugue in the Credo — singling, howling, stamping. After we had been listening a long time to this almost awful scene, and were about to go away, the door opened and Beethoven stood before us with distorted features, calculated to excite fear. He looked as if he had been in mortal combat with the whole host of contrapuntalists, his everlasting enemies. His first utterances were confused, as if he had been disagreeably surprised at our having overheard him. Then he reached the day's happenings and with obvious restraint he remarked: "Pretty doings, these, everybody has run away and I haven't had anything to eat since yesternoon!" I tried to calm him and helped him to make his toilet. My companion hurried on in advance to the restaurant of the bathing establishment to have something made ready for the famished master.

Eventually the word got out that Beethoven was writing again, and Vienna recovered some of its lapsed enthusiasm for its honored composer. Beethoven's symphonies began to turn up on Viennese concert programs; *Fidelio* was again revived; his quartets received renewed performances. The publication of the last piano sonatas occasioned great interest, although many people were completely mystified by Beethoven's new ecstatic musical language.

However, the greatest interest was aroused by the news that Beethoven had completed two immense orchestral works, one a Mass, the other a symphony. Vienna was dying to hear these works, especially when it was rumored that Beethoven was arranging to have them premiered in Berlin. In the winter of 1823–24, an appeal signed by thirty of Vienna's leading musicians appeared in the local press, encouraging Beethoven to mount his premieres there:

> Do not withhold longer from the popular enjoyment a performance of the latest masterworks of your hand. We know that a great sacred composition has been associated with that first one in which you have immortalized the emotions of a soul. . . . We know that a new flower glows in the garland of your glorious, still unequaled symphonies. For years, ever since the thunders of the victory at Vittoria ceased to reverberate, we have waited and hoped to see you distribute new gifts.

The upshot to this appeal was Beethoven's famous subscription concert of May 1824, his first in eleven years and, as it turned out, his last. At this concert, both excerpts from the *Missa Solemnis* and the entire Ninth Symphony were premiered. It has become one of the most famous evenings in musical history.

The Ninth Symphony represents everything that Beethoven stood for, both personally and musically, in his last years. It is an extraordinary achievement, both in its scope and in its tenacious and stubborn espousal of the ancient Enlightenment philosophy that would have in any other hands sounded impossibly false in the Europe of 1827. Beethoven had first considered setting Schiller's poem "Ode to Joy" as early as 1792; for thirty years the power of this hymn to freedom and joy had stayed with him. At the very end of his life, he presented his audiences with this summation of his personal and musical philosophy.

Beethoven and his friends had spent months organizing the concert, selecting soloists, engaging a choir and rehearsing the orchestra for this massive work. All Vienna was abuzz with anticipation. Although he did not conduct the orchestra, Beethoven was onstage to supervise the observance of tempi and dynamics, which he could do by watching the musicians closely.

The *Missa Solemnis*, first on the program, was a great success in the packed hall. The symphony received an ecstatic response. The second-movement scherzo was a sensation, interrupted by applause even as it was performed and occasioning an enormous ovation after its completion. It seemed the walls of the hall would shake and crumble at the din. Beethoven, however, his back to the audience, restlessly awaited the beginning of the next movement, unaware of the commotion. Finally, the alto soloist, realizing Beethoven's dilemma, plucked him by the sleeve and motioned him to turn around to receive his applause. The gesture galvanized the audience like an electric shock. The full poignancy of Beethoven's deafness had never been so powerfully demonstrated. He, who had created this magnificent music, had heard not a single note.

The concert of May 1824 was the last triumph of Beethoven's life.

Yet even it was soured by his now overpowering paranoia. The expenses for the concert were high and the receipts not as plentiful as he had expected. At a dinner held to celebrate the great success, Beethoven accused Schindler and others of having cheated him, and left the restaurant in a fury. It was several months before he realized that his suspicions were false and resumed relations with his former friends. They, by then, were familiar with this pattern of behavior.

Beethoven had finished writing his massive valedictory works by 1824. For the next three years, he concentrated all his compositional labors on five string quartets, each exemplifying the quiet, almost sublime spirituality of his late period. Musicians have puzzled over and thrilled to these quartets from the moment they first appeared. They represent the great composer's final message to us.

16

The Holy Song of Thanks: Op. 132

Beethoven's late interest in the string quartet was sparked by a commission he received in the early 1820s from a Russian nobleman, Prince Nicholas Galitzin, for three new quartets. In keeping with Beethoven's slower work pace in his later years, it was some time before he began the quartets, but once he did begin, he became completely absorbed in the project. Not only did he complete the three commissioned quartets, he kept going and wrote two more. These five works occupied him from the fall of 1824 to his death in the spring of 1827.

More has been written about these quartets than any other of Beethoven's late-period works, with the exception perhaps of the Ninth Symphony. Although different from one another, they share an air of mystery and spiritual depth. The quartet medium — four individual voices — has always lent itself to intimate musical thought, but Beethoven took that quality and magnified it tenfold in these last works.

As well, Beethoven continued to refine his musical language. The late quartets are allusive and elusive, hinting at musical ideas rather than fully developing them. The heroic bravery and exhibitionism that characterized the works of Beethoven's second period are gone now. A quieter, though still passionate, Beethoven has emerged.

The stylistic novelty of these quartets has led some commentators over the years to dismiss them as less than successful — music that has lost the ability to confront an audience directly and confidently. Different these works may be; unsuccessful they certainly are not. They explore different musical spaces than those of Beethoven's earlier works, but their craftsmanship and inspiration are equal to anything he wrote. We do, however, need to listen to them with an especially attentive ear.

The Quartet in A Minor, op. 132, was the second of the three Galitzin quartets. It was completed in mid-1825 and given an immediate and successful private performance for some of Beethoven's Vienna admirers. Of the final five quartets, it sits artistically somewhere in the middle. Not as gargantuan as op. 130, the third Galitzin quartet, it is also not as "experimental" as op. 131, Beethoven's seven-movement, penultimate work. Op. 132 will thus give us a chance to see Beethoven's late style as clearly as possible.

Using op. 132 as an introduction to the string quartet is a bit like learning to read with James Joyce's *Finnegan's Wake* — it's a complicated place to begin. So we need to preface our listening with a brief overview of the quartet form itself.

A string quartet is made up of four stringed instruments: two violins, a viola and a cello, representing the approximate ranges of the soprano, alto, tenor and bass human voices. However, unlike the varied colors of the orchestra, in which strings and winds, percussion and brass constantly enliven the texture of the music, the basic sound of the four stringed instruments in a quartet is quite homogeneous. Sometimes it is difficult to tell one instrument from the other — not just the two violins, which, of course, sound exactly the same, but even the viola or the cello, especially if they are playing in high registers. Don't worry if this is your experience. With very little practice, you will be able to separate the four voices easily.

Think of a quartet as a conversation between four extremely voluble people, who sometimes talk all at once and sometimes imitate, comment on or argue with one another. In a quartet, each line — each instrument — has an important role to play. The final texture is made up of four interweaving voices that can form themselves into a dizzying variety of combinations, all the while retaining their musical independence. Eventually, you'll be able to listen to all four lines of a quartet at the same time, although that may sound a bit like trying to watch each ring of a four-ring circus simultaneously. At first you might want to follow a single instrument (the first violin is usually the easiest), but soon you will be able to focus on the other instruments at the same time. The quartet texture will seem quite natural to you.

If the sound a string quartet produces is a little novel, the form in which a quartet is organized is not. All of Beethoven's eighteen quartets — from the earliest, written in 1800, to these last, written in the late 1820s — are in sonata form. You'll find the same pattern of exposition, development and recapitulation in their first movements, and combinations of theme and variations, minuet and trio and rondo finale in the following three. However, the sonata form Beethoven used in his late quartets is a far cry from the organization he had started with as a teenager in Bonn. Beethoven's new musical language bent sonata form profoundly in his last years, though never broke it.

What is new in the late quartets in the sparseness with which Beethoven develops the musical ideas contained in them. Beethoven's early and middle works are much more extroverted statements, intended for the stage of public performance. The late works are like interior monologues, in which the composer feels he need only hint at an idea to consider it exposed and remembered. The late works have a musical logic of their own.

The A-minor quartet is in five movements rather than the traditional four. Beethoven had begun to experiment with unusually numbered series of movements with the *Hammerklavier* Piano Sonata of

1817. In that massive work, the power and sublimity of the slow third movement required the addition of a transition movement before the finale, like a deep-sea diver returning from the ocean floor in stages rather than all at once. The same format is used here. An extra movement is added after the quartet's blissful slow movement and before the finale. Still, the overall sonata pattern of the work is basically maintained. The first movement, in sonata form, is followed by a sort of minuet and trio, then the slow movement and its following short march, and then a sonata finale.

Op. 132 begins with a slow introduction, the first one we have encountered in our listening. An intro is not that uncommon in sonata form. Composers often eased their audiences into their musical world with a slow introduction, like an overture to a musical or an opera. Traditionally, the music of the introduction was used as a throwaway and never referred to again in the piece.

Beethoven changed that practice early in his career. Never a composer to waste notes, Beethoven's intros are integral parts of the movements in which they appear. They not only set a mood, they often contribute to the musical ideas of the piece.

Such is the case here. This intro, with its close intervals, and air of mystery, immediately sets the work's tone and character. As well, the first four notes of this intro, played by the cello, will act as a main musical idea in this quartet, returning time and again, something like the drumroll motif at the beginning of the *Appassionata*.

That four-note motif is played four times, before the first violin suddenly breaks out of this eerie fog and leads to the introduction of the main theme of the first movement, played by the cello in a very high register.

This is less a theme than a musical fragment:

With a sort of rocking, syncopated rhythm, this idea is almost a prefix or suffix rather than a complete musical word. However, it will serve Beethoven as a basis for the entire movement, repeated again and again.

The first violin takes up the theme and extends it into a more complete phrase. Keep that opening rhythm in mind as you listen to this movement. As long as you can hear its pattern, you know you are in first-theme territory.

Were we back in the world of Beethoven's middle period, we would likely be swept away now by a cascading repetition of that rhythmic motif, ever increasing in power and intensity, à la the Fifth Symphony. However, as we are in the fragmentary world of the late Beethoven, that rhythmic figure is interrupted almost before it begins, after which the four-note motif from the introduction (or a form of it) returns, followed again by that wild descent in the first violin.

Although it sounds as though Beethoven has decided to start the piece over again, the return of the main motif, more fully developed this time, reminds us that we are still in the first-theme portion of the exposition. The continuity Beethoven was at such pains to establish in his heroic decade is less vital to him now. He is prepared to write discontinuous, almost disorienting moments — like this interruption in the midst of his first theme's development — as part of his new aesthetic.

This is music in which neat divisions of ideas into clear spaces has been replaced by a vision that is less linear but more integrated. It is as though all the musical ideas for the piece are present in Beethoven's mind simultaneously and can thus escape into the music at any moment. This kaleidoscopic character can eat away at the intelligibility of the form, because it threatens to destroy the unity of whatever section we happen to be in. That's not to say the late quartets lack meaning or even charm. They have both, plus a new quality of unpredictability that can be thrilling as well as mystifying. That's how they certainly appeared to many of Beethoven's contemporaries. Beethoven demands more from his listeners in these late works, because he is less interested in presenting clear, unequivocal statements of his musical thoughts than in exploiting their close interrelationship.

With the return of his first theme, Beethoven settles down into a section in which that theme is continually developed, even though its development now includes the unison arpeggiated figure that interrupted it in its first appearance. The rhythm of the first-theme fragment eventually gives way to a series of other ideas, any of which might serve as a second theme, but none of which does. Rather than tightly focus his melodic invention on one or two main packages, Beethoven in this quartet is quite lavish in his thematic largesse.

So we first hear a little melody in the first violin accompanied by chords off the beat in the other instruments; this quickly leads, via a unison passage of increasing intensity, to another tune begun by the first violin and then copied by cello and second violin, which also disappears as quickly as it appeared, giving way to a transition figure marked by a dotted rhythm in the first violin.

All this transition music scampers past us in a twinkling; one idea becomes the next without warning, and the effect is both powerful and disconcerting. This is the monologue aspect of the late works, the feeling that Beethoven is almost talking to himself in his music, not always taking the time to explain everything to his audience.

However, Beethoven has not abandoned the basic sonata pattern on which his whole creative life depended. Following that transition passage is a real second theme, in a new key and with a new musical focus. All the clues we have come to recognize as signifying a new idea are there. The accompaniment changes character and is now in triplets, and a new melody appears in the second violin, a quite lovely one:

Beethoven begins to develop this theme, but in keeping with his late style, the development doesn't last long. Almost immediately, all four instruments begin the coda with a series of quick ideas that alternate loud and soft, fast-moving and slow-moving passages, finally playing a series of detached notes that abruptly vanish into silence. The brooding four-note cello motif of the opening of the movement returns; the exposition is over.

This stop-and-start coda has been typical of the style of the movement so far, with a variety of highly condensed musical ideas following each other almost at random. The form, however, while stretched, is still recognizable. It is the first theme-second theme-coda pattern we have come to recognize as the exposition of a sonata. For all his terse musical phraseology, Beethoven has given us a formal framework we can follow.

The development section of the movement follows that quote from the slow introduction — no exposition repeat here. The first violin tentatively repeats the opening idea with its characteristic rhythm, then continues with the idea for several bars. The other instruments join in, with the most complete statement of that first theme yet, until the music is abruptly cut short by four notes played by all voices. Silence. Then the music gathers force again from a mini-melody played by cello and viola, before another four-note set brings the action to a halt a second time. Then, suddenly, like a flashback set in the middle of the development, all four instruments play the opening notes of the piece, that mysterious four-note motif.

The reappearance of this idea, played double-forte, is like an image that comes upon us in a dream, unbidden and unprepared for. The music is immediately shaken back to a sweet memory of its opening, with an elaborate version of the main theme given to the first violin, but this time the music of the slow intro, rather than disappearing, continues, and we hear both ideas together. Listen for that opening four-note idea, first in the cello at the very bottom of the texture, then in the first violin at the very top.

The memory of the exposition remains with the music as Beethoven, after a short passage, replays that wild first-violin line that introduced the main idea in the exposition and then proceeds with what sounds very much like the beginning of the piece. Although we are in a different key (you'll notice that everything sounds a little higher than it did at the opening), and the ideas are developed a bit more fully, this section of the development sounds suspiciously like a recapitulation. Rather than take small fragments of his exposition and develop them, as he did in his early career, Beethoven in this quartet develops the complete exposition as a whole.

Listen and you'll hear that all the pieces of the exposition fall into place in this developmental repeat, even if the pieces aren't exactly the same size. The main theme gives way to that descending unison arpeggio we heard at the beginning of the movement, followed by that quote from the slow four-note motif, elaborated here a bit, before returning to a development of the main theme, one more complex than we have yet heard. We keep expecting the music to take off in entirely new directions, as Beethoven might have done in earlier developments, but instead it sticks quite closely to the exposition pattern.

There's that first transition theme, the one in the first violin accompanied off the beat by the three supporting instruments, then the second, and the third, and before you know it, we're into a second version of the second theme. The music continues along the lines of the exposition, with much more elaboration and density but staying remarkably faithful to the pattern first established at the beginning of the piece. Beethoven has used his entire exposition as a theme for development.

When this development/recap reaches the point where the original exposition ended and the development began (a section introduced by four unison chords, then a repeat of the opening four-note motif), Beethoven extends the transition a few bars, but eventually follows suit and replays his main theme in the tonic key. The "real" recapitulation has begun.

However, Beethoven has not abandoned all of his previous musical thinking. After he's made such extensive use of his main theme in the development, the recapitulation must include some original material for the piece to maintain its forward flow. And so in this beginning of the recap, Beethoven actually borrows a few ideas he first introduced in the development to present his first theme. Then, a brand-new idea: a trill in the first violin and a descending scale played in individual notes by the rest of the ensemble. Is Beethoven about to give us something new?

Actually, no. This new idea merely introduces what we have called our second transition theme, which leads to the third and then a final statement of the second theme, now in A major.

Beethoven has now had enough of his "real" recapitulation, which he can cut short, of course, because he used so much of the material from the exposition in the development section. After the statement of the second theme, the movement's coda begins immediately. The first theme is quoted simply in the first violin and then, increasing in intensity and depth, by all the instruments. A few new phrases interspersed with quotes of the main theme lead us to a series of mysterious trills in the lower instruments, which are joined by the upper and a group of staccato chords in the lower strings played off against a repeated note in the first violin. The movement ends.

Beethoven has done some strange things to sonata form in this first movement, especially with its double recapitulation. The supremacy of the recapitulation — one recapitulation — in creating that all-important sense of return was one of the unchallenged maxims of sonata composition. Having the recap appear twice, in effect, seems to undermine the dramatic impact of the form. However, the late Beethoven was not after the same sort of dramatic effects he created in his early and middle works. What he was trying to achieve here was a greater sense of unity than was usual in a first movement, to create a form that was more organic and less sectional. The repeated return of the music of the first thematic area provides a sense of continuity that balances the abrupt terseness of the musical ideas themselves. Beethoven was a sonata man to the end, casting his thoughts, no matter how novel, in the familiar pattern of home-away-home. However, he constantly found new ways to make that traditional pattern fresh and original. The double recapitulation of the first movement of op. 132 is a case in point, as are similar innovations in the following movements.

The second movement of op. 132 is a traditional minuet and trio, if anything in the late Beethoven can be called traditional. The minuet is based on two simple musical ideas, which are presented at the beginning of the movement: a two-bar accompaniment figure of two upward triads, which is what you hear as the movement begins, and a little melody that follows in the first violin.

No two ideas could seem simpler, but notice how they contradict each other rhythmically. The accents in the accompaniment fall on the first and fourth beats of the phrase, but in the second idea they are on the first and fifth beats. Beethoven loved creating these rhythmic puzzles, and the entire first section of this movement is taken up with the delicious possibilities these cross-rhythms allow.

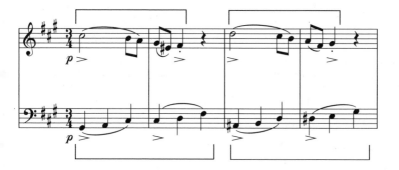

The entire minuet is made up of only these two phrases and fragments in dozens of ever-changing rhythmic and harmonic combinations. As is often the case in these late works, a musical idea that Beethoven previously would have used, developed and then dropped takes on something of an obsessive character. Rather than being part of a developing musical structure, the repeated ideas seem to be used for their sound alone, like the repetition of a word over and over again until it loses its meaning and becomes mere sound. In several of his late works, Beethoven uses the trill — traditionally an ornament of another note — as a musical element in itself. In his last piano sonata, pages of trills follow one another, becoming musical ideas rather than musical tricks. The same thing is at work in this minuet.

The minuet itself is quite long, made up of two sections, each of which is repeated. The first of the two sections is simpler and more straightforward, the second more complex. A coda brings the minuet to a graceful close. Then Beethoven gives us a bit of pure musical fun.

In contrast to the almost obsessive character of the minuet, Beethoven creates in the trio one of his most delightful and down-to-earth musical moments. Echoes of folk music often appear in the late works, which, for all their sublimity, make frequent use of the most rustic musical ideas. This trio is one of them.

As the minuet ends, we are immediately transported to a country party, or so it seems. That is definitely a hurdy-gurdy Beethoven is imitating in the first violin, complete with its bagpipe-like drone and its utterly charming melody. A country dance begins, with all four instruments taking a turn, the viola especially cutting quite a figure. This is the world that Beethoven visited all those summers in the country; it is the world of the "rude mechanicals" of Shakespeare's *A Midsummer Night's Dream*. One almost expects to see Bottom the tailor leap to the dance floor.

However, this setting is not continued forever. The festive mood is suddenly interrupted by, of all things, the beginning of the four-note motif that we heard way back at the beginning of the first movement! It is as though a character from act 1 of this musical drama has been dragged onto the dance floor in act 2. It is an audacious connection between two movements and two moods, which provides us with a good deal of surprise in just ten seconds of music. However, the interruption is short; the rustic dance reappears, closes off, and then, true to form, the minuet returns to end the movement.

If there is a major formal shift in Beethoven's late works, it is in the prominence and musical significance given to their slow movements. At the beginning of his career, Beethoven placed most of the musical emphasis on the first movement of his sonata works, as was the custom. One of the defining features of his second period, on the other hand, was his increasing emphasis on the final movement of works, on endings rather than beginnings. The drama of his second period was founded on this principle. Now, at the end of his life, it is the slow, middle movements that carry increasing musical weight. In the late works, the slow movement is often the musical center of the piece, as it is here.

The slow movement of op. 132 is unusual, even for late Beethoven. It is based on a chorale, a sort of hymn used in German liturgy to express the simplest, most heartfelt religious sentiments. Its title explains why Beethoven chose this form for the movement. He called it "A Holy Song of Thanks of a convalescent to the Godhead, in the Lydian mode." Beethoven had been ill in the early part of 1825 and had recovered, so the movement has an obvious autobiographical reference. However, even without the title, the movement's intent is clear. It radiates a kind of divine peace and repose, a moment when the spiritual character of Beethoven's late works is most obvious.

The Lydian mode referred to in Beethoven's title is one of the old scales used in the Middle Ages, before major and minor scales came to dominate Western music. Beethoven had researched these scales in preparation for the *Missa Solemnis*. The use of the mode here enhances the medieval, mystical character of the movement.

In keeping with the movement's unique character, Beethoven created a special form for it as well. The heart of the movement is the chorale, a slow-moving, hymnlike theme played by all four instruments in lockstep. The chorale returns, in one form or another, three times during the movement. Between the chorale sections Beethoven twice interspersed a section he headed in the score "With a feeling of new strength," a frisky, joyful portrait of an invalid returning to life. These five sections make up the formal structure of the movement.

However, in his chorale sections Beethoven does not just present the hymn in an uninterrupted fashion. He breaks the chorale up into five short sections, each preceded by a sort of introduction, played slightly faster by the four instruments.

The movement begins with one of these introductory sections. The first violin starts alone, followed in turn by each of the other instruments in a short, scene-setting moment. Then the chorale itself begins, a wonderfully peaceful, timeless melody. The chorale's first phrase comes to a gentle end, and the second introductory section begins, again led by the first violin. The second chorale section follows this second introduction. Five times in all, an introductory section precedes a phrase of the chorale, until the first section of the movement comes to a close. We have spent a timeless moment in religious contemplation.

Then, in a twinkling, the mood changes, and a happy, almost

playful section begins with a trill in the first violin and a melody in the second. This is the section Beethoven headed in the score "With a feeling of new strength." In it Beethoven suggests that wonderful moment when an invalid realizes that health has returned and life has new meaning. The portrayal of this simple joy is one of Beethoven's most successful musical portraits and provides a perfect balance to the reverential solemnity of the opening chorale. This section continues for a page or two, with the two violins tossing ideas back and forth like a game of catch. Finally, the first violin takes over with a lyrical melody, and the section comes to a mysterious and abrupt end, vanishing as quickly as it appeared. Never had Beethoven contrasted two ideas and moods more completely.

With the end of this intermezzo, we move back to the chorale. We hear the solo violin begin this section as it began the movement, with a brief introduction to the chorale proper. However, this time Beethoven increases the emotional intensity of the chorale by combining it with the introductory sections, mixing and blending the two textures. The introductory section begins as it did before, but when the chorale enters — in the first violin — the other three voices continue with their commentary. The texture, which had been so spare in the first section, is now rich and emotional. The five sections of the chorale still appear as they did before — listen for them in the first violin only — but they are now embedded in a warmer, more comforting musical community.

This section finally comes to a conclusion with the last phrase of the chorale and is followed again by the same section that followed it last time, the return-to-strength section. The section is embellished now as well; if anything, it is more frisky and springlike. It continues just as it did before (there is virtually no thematic development in this movement), and we return for the last time to the serenity of the chorale.

In this last journey through the chorale, Beethoven varies his approach yet again. We noted how the introductory sections took on added life in the second version of the chorale. In this third version, those sections become the main musical event, with the chorale itself relegated somewhat to the background. The effect is to heighten the emotional charge of the chorale section until it reaches an almost unparalleled intensity.

Up to now this movement has increased in strength and power as it has progressed. The spare character of the opening has given way to increasingly elaborate music in each succeeding section, and this final section seems no exception. As it begins, the introductory music is further intensified with an instruction for the performers to play "with the most intimate feeling." However, as the section continues, Beethoven achieves a miraculous effect: the music slows and slows, as though it were evaporating in the heat of a too powerful emotion. By the end of this final chorale section, the music has almost completely vanished; the movement ends with a chord played on the highest notes in each instrument's range, as softly as possible. Beethoven has sent his music soaring into the cosmos.

One can imagine the reaction of audiences in 1825 to this kind of ecstatic song. Even today, when we have been exposed to music expressing the widest range of feeling, this movement is still unique, as expressionistic as anything any twentieth-century composer ever attempted. Beethoven created a world in this movement we now associate with all his late works, a form of musical communion that has never really been emulated.

However, something has to follow this ineffable third movement, and Beethoven's instincts told him it would be impossible to launch right into the finale after such an intense musical experience. So he provides something of an entr'acte: a sprightly little march, a perfect antidote to the sublimity of what has gone before. Everything here is regular and square, although Beethoven can't resist a little rhythmic joke from time to time by displacing the accents of the theme.

Nonetheless, the march proceeds nicely toward what should be a trio section, but instead Beethoven writes a little scene for the first violin that might have come out of an opera. The violin makes an extravagant musical statement above tremolo strings, launches into a quick scale run, and the movement poises on the brink of the finale. Beethoven needs this section, because the march is not really a full movement at all but an extended bridge to get us from the contemplative mood of the third movement to the genial mood of the finale.

Compared with the complexities of the first movement and the depths of the third, the finale of op. 132 is more accessible and comforting. Originally planned as the last movement of the Ninth Symphony (before Beethoven decided to put the "Ode to Joy" there instead), this finale with its charming opening melody has the character of a folk song.

The movement is in rondo form, with a recurring main theme, similar to the structure of *Für Elise*. The opening idea, the one that returns several times within the movement, is set out clearly at the beginning, played by the first violin. It is a dancelike tune that sets up the good-natured character of the entire movement.

The key to hearing the form of this movement is listening for the return of that first musical theme. We hear it at the opening, when it is followed by contrasting musical ideas (something like a second-theme area in a sonata exposition). The next time it returns, the material that follows is different and more dramatic (like a development section). The third appearance of the theme functions like a recapitulation, with the following material the same as at the opening. Finally, the last mention of the theme is in a furious coda, in which Beethoven doubles the speed of his instruments to create a satisfying close to the movement and the work, ending in a brilliant A major rather than the sombre A minor in which it began.

Because the structure of this movement has characteristics of both rondo and sonata form, it is called a sonata-rondo, a form used for many final movements in the classical literature and somewhat easier to follow than strict sonata movements. After all the demands this quartet has placed on its listeners, Beethoven felt the need to end with a simpler movement, one that could balance the emotion of the earlier parts of the work without sacrificing any of its integrity.

Like all of his late works, this A-minor string quartet is both a puzzle and an extraordinary artistic experience. Beethoven has packed so many contradictory moods into the work — the somber opening, the hurdy-gurdy festivities of the second movement, the churchlike solemnity of the third movement and the bucolic moments of the fifth movement — that it threatens to fly apart in a welter of unsympathetic parts. But it does hang together, precisely because its wide range of emotions matches the states of consciousness we can imagine its author experiencing. The late works are a portrait of an extremely rich soul in close-up. Even if they give voice to feelings we have not ourselves experienced, we can, by proxy, share in their reflected grace. They are not as accessible and as welcoming as Beethoven's earlier works, but for many listeners they represent the composer at his most complete and profound.

Beethoven's life was entering its last phase when he wrote op. 132 and the quartets that followed. But the resting place he had found in his music was not to be echoed in his life. There was one final drama to play out.

17

The Last Movement

Beethoven began the last chapter of his life in a calmer state than he had experienced for years. The stormy turbulence of the custody dispute was behind him, and his life, if not settled (Beethoven's life was never settled), was at least superficially more placid.

Better relations with his nephew contributed much to this new sense of peace. Problems with Karl had largely evaporated by 1820, when the custody issue was settled and Beethoven returned to his work. Beethoven even made friendly overtures to Johanna in the early 1820s, but, as always, suspicion clouded his mind after each tentative gesture, and the doors to reconciliation, opened a crack, were invariably slammed shut. In any case, neither Beethoven's more amicable relations with Karl nor his tentative reconciliation with Johanna was to last. The Karl story had not reached its climax.

Karl van Beethoven was nearly twenty in 1825 and had been working on his studies in a consistent, if unspectacular, manner. About to finish school, he was beginning to think of a career. Like any young man, he valued his freedom and, as he matured, demanded more of it. More, however, his uncle was not willing to grant. Perhaps fearful of Karl leaving him for good, or anxious about the young man's developing sexuality, Beethoven kept his nephew on the shortest possible leash. Money was doled out to him in niggardly amounts, and an intricate accounting of every penny was demanded. Beethoven constantly questioned Karl's friends and servants about his movements and even paid one to spy on the young man. Beethoven was worried that Karl might be gambling or spending too much on luxuries.

Inevitably, the young man chafed at these restrictions, which seem to have depressed him considerably. Just as surely, Beethoven interpreted Karl's impatience as a betrayal, one engineered by Johanna. The recriminations continued in the summer and fall of 1825. In July, upon hearing that Karl had been seeing Johanna once again, he wrote:

> Until now [it was] only conjecture although someone assured me that there were secret dealings again between you and your mother — Am I to experience once again the most abominable ingratitude? No, if this bond is to be broken, so be it, but you will be despised by all impartial men who hear of this ingratitude. . . . Shall I get involved again in these vulgarities? No, never again — in God's name if the Pactum weighs upon you — I turn you over to Divine Providence. I have done my job and upon this I can appear before the mightiest of all judges.

A week later, he added:

> God is my witness, I only dream of being completely removed from you and from this wretched brother and this abominable family to which I am attached — God grant me my wish, for I cannot trust you any more —
>
> *Unfortunately your Father or better not your Father*

As always, Beethoven felt remorseful the minute he sent one of these letters and immediately sought reconciliation with his nephew. As for poor Karl, it is hard to imagine which would have been more distressing, the blasts of anger or the pathetic pleas for forgiveness that inevitably followed. This letter was sent in October of 1825:

My precious son!
Go no further — Come but to my arms, not a harsh word shall you hear. O God, do not rush away in your misery. You will be received as lovingly as ever. What to consider, what to do in the future, these things we will talk over affectionately. On my word of honour, no reproaches. . . . Do but come — Come to the faithful heart of

your father Beethoven

Come home immediately upon receiving this. Only for God's sake come back home today. It might bring you who knows what danger. Hurry, hurry.

In the early months of 1826, the situation with Karl began to take an ominous turn. Many commentators believe that the letter just quoted was written to forestall a desperate act on Karl's part. There is no doubt that the possibility of suicide had entered the young man's mind by 1826; the Conversation Books are full of discussions between Beethoven and his closest friends on this matter. It is hard to know exactly what changed for Karl in the early months that year to lead him to this critical point. Final exams were approaching at the university; he may have amassed severe gambling debts; his uncle was an increasing burden. In any case, emotions began building in Karl that he felt powerless to control.

Finally, he took matters into his own hands. On the evening of July 29, 1826, Karl bought two pistols and drove out into the country. He spent the night writing letters and then, early in the morning, pressed the two guns to his head. One bullet missed entirely; the other grazed his scalp but remained lodged in his head. A passerby noticed the wounded youth, who asked that he be taken to his mother's house.

It was thus Johanna who first informed Beethoven of the tragedy that had befallen them both. Karl was not fatally wounded but would need several months of convalescence. Beethoven was shattered. As Stephan von Breuning's son, Gerhard, wrote:

> The pain which he received from this attempt was indescribable; he was cast down as a father who has lost his much-loved son. My mother met him on the Glacis completely undone. "Do you know what has happened? My Karl has shot himself." "And — is he dead?" "No, it was a glancing shot, he is still living, there's hope that he can be saved; but the disgrace that he has brought upon me; and I loved him so."

Although there was much sympathy for Beethoven in the aftermath of the suicide attempt, there was condemnation as well. Many factors undoubtedly led Karl to try to take his own life, but when asked, he pointed an accusing finger at his uncle. As attempted suicide was a crime in Vienna, Karl was brought to trial. The explanation he gave the examining magistrate was that Beethoven "tormented [me] too much. I grew worse because my uncle wanted me to be better." A friend of Beethoven's, Karl Holz, interviewed Karl and reported back to the composer: "He said he was tired of life, because he saw in it something different from what you judiciously and righteously could approve."

Overnight, according to one report, Beethoven looked like a man of seventy, his once proud figure bowed and broken as he made his way through Vienna. Nonetheless, plans needed to be made for Karl upon his release from hospital. In the months leading up to his suicide attempt, Karl had expressed interest in pursuing a military career, but

Beethoven had categorically rejected this option. Now, however, spurred on by Stephan von Breuning, who worked in the Austrian war department, Beethoven relented, and arrangements were made for Karl to join a regiment in the winter of 1826, as soon as his health would permit. If Karl's suicide attempt was intended to free him, one way or another, from the domination of his uncle, it had achieved its effect. Beethoven realized that his overpowering control over his nephew had to end.

To complete Karl's convalescence, Beethoven accepted an invitation to visit his brother Johann and his wife on their country estate near Gneixendorf in October. In previous years Beethoven had reacted to Johann's wife, Therese, just as he had to Carl's wife, Johanna. In 1812 he had tried to get the police to remove Therese from Linz, where she had been living with Johann, to prevent the couple from marrying. However, Beethoven had later dropped his opposition to the match, so a visit with them now seemed like a good idea. Although the original plans were that Beethoven and Karl would stay only a week, their trip was extended for several months, through the fall of 1826 and winter of 1826–27.

A reconciliation between Beethoven and his nephew, badly needed, seems to have taken root in the country air of Gneixendorf, and Beethoven spent a few idyllic weeks there. Unfortunately, relations between the Beethoven brothers were not as harmonious. Both had begun their sojourn together with the best of intentions, but the bitter habits of a lifetime are not easily broken. Eventually, Beethoven again soured on Therese and made his displeasure known to his brother. Things came to a head when Beethoven demanded that Johann cut Therese out of his will and leave everything he had to Karl. Johann naturally refused, and Beethoven, in a rage, gathered Karl up and headed back to Vienna. It was a cold December first, and during the frantic trip home in an open coach Beethoven caught pneumonia. On his arrival in Vienna, he was sent straight to bed.

Beethoven never recovered his health. Although he survived the pneumonia, his weakened condition made him vulnerable to a host of other illnesses, mainly diseases of the liver, which finally overcame him within a few weeks. Beethoven had never been a healthy man. One history of his illnesses fills twenty-five pages. Along with the deafness that had plagued him for thirty years, Beethoven had suffered continuing bowel problems and indigestion as well as bouts of smallpox, typhus, pneumonia, eye trouble and other assorted ailments. Medical science in the early 1800s was primitive; nothing was understood about germs, the chemical composition of the body or the cause of disease. Many of the treatments Beethoven was prescribed had not changed substantially since the Middle Ages. There is hardly a single medical procedure to which he was subjected that one can confidently say was effective. In many cases the treatment probably made his condition worse.

But until the winter of 1826–27, Beethoven had always managed to get the better of his many illnesses. Now his body was worn out. After the pneumonia passed, dropsy developed. Dropsy, a symptom rather than a disease itself, occurs when the body retains abnormal amounts of water. The best treatment is to attack the underlying cause, which is either poor circulation or a virus affecting the kidneys or liver. Unfortunately, none of this was known to medical science in 1827, and all Beethoven's doctors could do was drain off the excess fluid in his body by means of a procedure known as tapping. This process relieves the internal pressure but does nothing to attack the cause. Beethoven was tapped four times between early December 1826 and late February 1827, but his liver disease, left untreated, continued to sap his strength. Some days he would recover his spirits and be cheerful, but most of the time he slept. After the fourth tapping had brought no change in his condition, Beethoven knew he was finished. He renewed his will, making Karl his sole heir, tried to tidy up his business affairs and said his last farewells to his friends and acquaintances.

During his last few weeks, Beethoven became better acquainted with the works of Franz Schubert and received a complete edition of the works of Handel, which gave him great pleasure. An honorarium from the London Philharmonic Society of 100 pounds touched him deeply.

On March 23, 1827, he lapsed into a coma, and then on March 26, with Schindler and von Breuning out looking for a grave site, he died. Beethoven had been left in the care of Anselm Hüttenbrenner, a friend of Schubert's, and a woman Hüttenbrenner claimed was Johanna van Beethoven. His account has been often quoted:

> Frau van Beethoven and I only were in the death-chamber during the last moments of Beethoven's life. After Beethoven had lain unconscious, the death-rattle in his throat from 3 o'clock in the afternoon till after 5, there came a flash of lightning accompanied by a violent clap of thunder, which garishly illuminated the death-chamber. (Snow lay before Beethoven's dwelling.) After this unexpected phenomenon of nature, which startled me greatly, Beethoven opened his eyes, lifted his right hand and looked up for several seconds with his fist clenched and a very serious, threatening expression as if he wanted to say: "Inimical powers, I defy you! Away with you! God is with me!" It also seemed as if, like a brave commander, he wished to call out to his wavering troops: "Courage, soldiers! Forward! Trust in me! Victory is assured!" When he let the raised hand sink to the bed, his eyes closed halfway. My right hand was under his head, my left rested on his breast. Not another breath, not a heartbeat more! The genius of the great master of tones fled from this world of delusion into the realm of truth.

Beethoven was fifty-six when he died. If indeed Johanna van Beethoven was with the composer at his deathbed (Hüttenbrenner later changed his mind and identified Therese van Beethoven as the companion), we may suppose that Beethoven left this life reconciled with the woman who had haunted and obsessed him for a decade. In any case, Frau van Beethoven, either Johanna or Therese, took a lock of the composer's hair for a keepsake (a lock which was rediscovered in 1994), and Beethoven was allowed his final rest. A life of great tumult and torment had come to an end.

Beethoven's funeral was a major event in Vienna. Twenty thousand people either crowded into the courtyard of his last apartment, lined the route to the church or followed the funeral procession to the grave site. All Vienna's notables — musicians, artists and aristocrats — were among the mourners. Famous musicians were pallbearers; a leading poet, Franz Grillparzer, wrote a funeral oration, which was performed by one of Vienna's leading actors. Beethoven's fame, which had taken root in the aristocratic circles of the Austrian capital in the last decade of the eighteenth century, had reached international proportions by the time he died. Unlike Mozart, buried in a pauper's grave in the same Vienna thirty-five years earlier, mourned by none but his wife and a few friends, Beethoven went to his final resting place acknowledged by Grillparzer as "the last master of tuneful song, the organ of soulful concord, the heir and amplifier of Handel and Bach's, of Haydn and Mozart's immortal fame." He had become a world figure in his lifetime.

It is a measure of Beethoven's extraordinary achievement that more than 150 years later, his fame is greater than ever. The normal currents of time have not eroded his musical reputation. If anything, it stands today more honored than ever. Changes of musical style and taste have not affected him. From romanticism to late romanticism to impressionism, atonality, neoclassicism and new romanticism, Beethoven's integrity remains uncorrupted. Although many other composers from the past are still honored today, only Beethoven can boast an uninterrupted reputation from his own time to ours.

Since Beethoven's music has been with us for more than two centuries, you might think we would have discovered by now exactly what makes it so enduringly popular. Well, we haven't, really. The best we can do is note its power and marvel at its ability to speak so directly and personally to its audiences. Beethoven's music is extremely well-balanced, combining great simplicity of musical material with great sophistication in its manipulation. It is both spontaneously emotional and controlled by strict formal design; it is personal and universal at the same time.

For musicians, Beethoven has had a monumental impact. No composer since has been able to escape the force of his music. Franz Liszt invoked Old Testament imagery to explain Beethoven's influence: "To us musicians the work of Beethoven parallels the pillars of smoke and fire which led the Israelites through the desert. . . . His darkness and his light equally trace for us the road we must follow; both the one and the other are a perpetual commandment, an infallible revelation."

The power of Beethoven's music, while unavoidable, has not always been welcomed by later musicians. The heroic dimensions of his achievement have given pause to generations of future composers. Schubert was the first composer of genius to be awed by Beethoven. Decades later, Johannes Brahms could explain his reluctance to compose a symphony by referring to Beethoven: "You don't know what it's like to hear the tramp of a giant behind you." Beethoven gave to music a new tension and intensity that remained every composer's legacy.

Beethoven not only expanded the emotional range of music, he was a great master of musical technique, on both the small and the large scale. For more than a century, his combination of imagination and craftsmanship provided musicians with models that demonstrated the intimate relationship of form to content. Beethoven's scores have thus been studied by composers whose styles have differed enormously from his. Arnold Schoenberg, at the beginning of this century, writing music that Beethoven would likely have considered sheer noise, cited the *Eroica* Symphony as a major influence, because in it, Schoenberg explained, Beethoven taught him not to waste a single note.

Beethoven was more than a master craftsman and a powerful musical presence. His music, and especially that of his second, heroic period, embodies in sound the political and social ideals of the world in which he lived. By capturing them in his music he has delivered them right to our very doorstep, with a freshness and innocence that two hundred years of history have denied us in the real world. If today we believe a little less surely in our intrinsic ability to fashion a completely new world and to live together in harmony, Beethoven's music reminds us of the purity of those original ideals and the possibility of recovering them. It is inspirational music in the truest sense of the word. The fact that Beethoven's music still speaks to our jaded late twentieth-century sensibility proves that those ideals were not just products of a certain period in European history but have become part of humanity's common heritage of hope.

Beethoven the man is a more ambiguous figure than Beethoven the composer. If his works shine in their purity, his life is full of contradictions. Whereas earlier generations found these contrasts inexplicable, we today are more understanding. We know that in artistic personalities darkness and light go hand in hand. Many people would have been defeated by the dark, barren forces arrayed against Beethoven, yet he persevered. Neither deafness, poor health, loneliness nor his psychological torments could entirely deaden the creative life within him. In both his music and his life, Beethoven was constantly alive, looking to the future, to the next project. Right to the end he was thinking fresh and original musical thoughts, challenging himself time and time again. This sense of challenge is a key characteristic of Beethoven's art. The beauty in his music is the beauty of achievement, of overcoming adversity, a triumph we all share as listeners. We love Beethoven's music because he has given us these overheard victories, which become our own.

We may be sceptical of heroes in our emerging postmodern world, and Beethoven is an easy target for those who wish to adopt a cooler, more balanced approach to the history of Western art. His mythic quality may strike some as overblown. However, it is a mistake to see in Beethoven merely the limited cultural aspirations of a generation long past. Beethoven, as much if not more so than any other musician in our cultural history, believed in the universality of art, in its power to form bridges between people and nations. His music was written for everyone to hear, understand and appreciate. And with just a little practice, you can bring his art into your life and experience it as millions before you have done. As you enter Beethoven's world, music's electrical current, which connects people separated by time, space and culture, will spark into existence once again.

Appendix
Beethoven's Top Forty

Symphonies

Symphony no. 1 in C Major, op. 21

Beethoven's First Symphony is set firmly within the traditions established by Haydn and Mozart. Composed in 1800, it was one of Beethoven's first attempts to spread his artistic wings beyond the confines of the piano sonata. Although much of the work could have been composed by Mozart (hardly a devastating criticism), there are many pure Beethoven touches. The introduction to the symphony is in the wrong key, the violins can't seem to make up their minds to begin the final movement, and the minuet has the kind of rushing motif that Beethoven was to use in many symphonies to follow. Although able to stand on its own two artistic feet, the First Symphony is still most interesting as a contrast to Beethoven's symphonic efforts of only a few years later.

Symphony no. 2 in D Major, op. 36

The Second Symphony was written during the Heiligenstadt summer but betrays not the slightest trace of the testament's despair. Instead, high spirits and an almost adolescent clownishness characterize a work filled with the brightest of melodies and moments of fun. The last movement is especially exuberant, with a theme that could accompany a children's pantomime. Each of the four movements of the Second Symphony represents an advance on its counterpart in the First. The sonata form of the first movement is handled with greater dramatic flair, the melody of the slow, second movement is sweeter, the minuet and trio sprightlier and the finale more boisterous. All the works of the Heiligenstadt summer — this symphony, the opus 31 piano sonatas and the opus 30 violin sonatas — show Beethoven on the brink of the breakthrough represented by the *Eroica* Symphony. Confidence and growing assurance speak through every bar. No wonder the grief over his deafness spilled over into such despair only a few weeks after this symphony was written.

Symphony no. 3 in E-flat Major, op. 55 (*Eroica*)

See chapter 9.

Symphony no. 4 in B-flat Major, op. 60

If there could be such a thing as an obscure Beethoven symphony, the Fourth would be it. Sandwiched between the enormous Third and passionate Fifth, the Fourth Symphony has suffered in comparison with its neighbors. Written in 1806, the Fourth would be a masterwork by any composer other than the one who had written the *Eroica* three years earlier. Where the earlier symphony had broken new musical ground, the Fourth seems to return to more familiar terrain and loses a bit as a result. Not that it doesn't have its wonderful moments, particularly the lengthy slow introduction and quirky third-movement minuet. But the comic-opera flavor of the final movement and regular phraseology of the first rob the symphony of a place in the first rank of Beethoven's orchestral compositions.

Symphony no. 5 in C Minor, op. 67

The Fifth Symphony is Beethoven's most famous composition and has been so almost from its premiere in 1808. The "knock of Fate" with which it begins is the best-known bit of classical music ever written, used in countless cartoons and comedies, as well as by the Allied forces in the Second World War as a symbol of resistance. (The four notes of the opening tap out the Morse code for V.) The first movement of the symphony is almost entirely based on the rhythm of its opening four notes, spun out over five hundred bars in ever-increasing excitement. The second movement is a theme and variations, and the third a mysterious scherzo featuring pizzicato notes in the strings. The third movement immediately opens onto the finale, a triumphant march in C major. The Fifth Symphony is like the *Moonlight* Sonata in that the familiarity of its first movement can obscure for listeners the fact that it ends in a dramatically different mood. Never before had Beethoven moved so consciously from tension to resolution as he did in this work. In the words of E.T.A. Hoffmann's famous review, the symphony "induces terror, fright, horror and pain and awakens that endless longing which is the essence of romanticism."

Symphony no. 6 in F Major, op. 68 (*Pastoral*)

Beethoven worked on his Sixth Symphony at the same time as his Fifth and premiered them together at his famous concert of December 1808. Nonetheless, no two of his symphonies are more different. This serene Sixth is worlds apart from the passion of its mate. Subtitled "Pastoral symphony, or a recollection of country life," the symphony conjures up the joy Beethoven felt all his life in natural settings. Each of the movements has a heading, from the "Cheerful impressions on arriving in the country" of the first movement to the "Shepherd's Hymn" of the last. Although Beethoven claimed he had composed "more an expression of feeling than a painting," the *Pastoral* stands as the first tone-poem in modern musical history. Dozens of works describing battles, stories and natural scenes written over the next hundred years trace their lineage to this work, although few of them follow the strict sonata form Beethoven employed here. The *Pastoral* represents a "road not taken" for Beethoven, a glimpse at the composer he might have become had he been won over to full-fledged romanticism.

Symphony no. 7 in A Major, op. 92

Richard Wagner called the Seventh Symphony "the apotheosis of the dance," and dancelike rhythms inspire each movement of this work, which Beethoven completed just before his letter to the Immortal Beloved in 1812. With its inexhaustible energy, the Seventh is more frenetic than either the Fifth or the Third Symphony, its two closest companions. The slow movement is a theme and variations like that of the *Appassionata* Sonata, simple yet moving. The finale bursts forth in a rhythmic blaze and never lowers the temperature. The Seventh is Beethoven's most energetic and hypnotic symphony.

Symphony no. 8 in F Major, op. 93

Like the Fifth and Sixth Symphonies, the Seventh and Eighth were composed together and also differ dramatically in mood and texture. The Eighth sees Beethoven in a quieter mood, almost a throwback to the more refined texture Mozart and Haydn had created for their symphonies a generation earlier. Beethoven simplified his style in the Eighth in an attempt to find a new path through sonata form. The second-movement allegretto is supposed to be an imitation of Maelzel's recently invented metronome, and the final allegro contains some of Beethoven's most obvious musical jokes. An unjustly neglected work.

Symphony no. 9 in D Minor, op. 125 (*Choral*)

The Ninth is Beethoven's most massive symphony, monumental both in size and in artistic vision. Several years in gestation, the Ninth represents one of Beethoven's artistic pinnacles, a prolonged hymn to brotherhood and joy. Each of the work's four movements dwarfs all its predecessors. In the first movement, Beethoven represents musically the birth of the cosmos, a universe coming together slowly but with terrific force. The second-movement scherzo, with its opening D-minor triad split between strings and tympani, created a sensation at the premiere and had to be encored. The slow, third movement is a languid theme and variations that opens up an idyllic world of peace and relaxation after the storms of the first two movements. However, the key to the symphony is its final movement, a setting of Schiller's "Ode to Joy," which adds vocal soloists and chorus to the symphony orchestra. Beethoven had considered setting Schiller's ode as early as 1792 but waited thirty years to carry out his goal. The finale to the Ninth expresses Beethoven's personal philosophy more clearly than anything else he wrote. Its combination of joy in brotherhood and humility before God is as inspiring today as it was in 1824. Challenging and complex, the Ninth is Beethoven's valedictory, a summation of a lifetime of writing for the orchestra.

Concertos

Piano Concerto no. 1 in C Major, op. 15

The C Major Concerto was actually the second Beethoven wrote but the first to be published. Like the First Symphony, also in C major, the first concerto is a careful attempt by Beethoven to familiarize himself with the medium. Securely set within the traditions of concerto writing established by Mozart, the C Major Concerto nonetheless has many touches only Beethoven could provide. The final-movement rondo is especially joyous, with Beethoven in the best musical mood of his entire career. Listen to the boisterous succession of themes in this last movement and you can imagine the rough, country playfulness of a young man increasingly confident of his ability, not yet troubled by the shadow of deafness. Beethoven's natural good humor shines through this work.

Piano Concerto no. 2 in B-flat Major, op. 19

Written before the C Major Concerto but published after it, the B-flat Concerto is not one of Beethoven's most distinguished works. Here Mozart is a model to be slavishly followed rather than a point of departure. An exception is the final movement of the work, added later, which uses syncopated off-beats to create some of the same energy we hear in the finale to the C Major Concerto.

Piano Concerto no. 3 in C Minor, op. 37

Poised on the threshold of his second period, the third concerto (1800) was Beethoven's first completely successful orchestral composition. In contrast to the first two concertos, the writing here is assured and original, with a command that would turn up again in the *Eroica* a couple of years later. A spare first movement is followed by one of Beethoven's loveliest slow movements, and an energetic rondo finale concludes the work. Beethoven often performed this concerto in Vienna, always with great success.

Piano Concerto no. 4 in G Major, op. 58

The G Major is Beethoven's first great second-period concerto. Unique from first note to last, the fourth concerto belongs to that group of more reflective works that Beethoven composed after completing his opera, *Fidelio*. It opens with the solo piano announcing the main theme, which is then taken up by the orchestra, kicking off a work that constantly breaks the rules of normal concerto writing. The most original part of the piece is its dramatic second movement, in which the solo piano and the strings of the orchestra engage in an impassioned dialogue, trading phrases back and forth for several pages. The final rondo begins in the wrong key (a favorite Beethoven joke) and rushes to a powerful conclusion. The fourth may be Beethoven's most perfect concerto.

Piano Concerto no. 5 in E-flat Major, op. 73 (*Emperor*)

Unlike the contemplative fourth, the *Emperor* Concerto is a work written on a grand, public scale. Rather than opening with a quiet statement of the theme, the fifth begins with a powerful series of chords played by orchestra and soloist in alternation. The *Emperor* was composed in 1809, just as Beethoven's heroic passion was beginning to fade, and although the concerto contains many passages of great beauty, Beethoven seems unable to sustain his inspiration throughout the entire piece. Every so often the work lapses into repetitive phrases that lack the imaginative brilliance of his earlier compositions. After the *Emperor*, Beethoven entered a sterile period that did not really end for almost a decade.

Violin Concerto in D Major, op. 61

Beethoven's single violin concerto was not very popular in his lifetime, although it is a staple of the repertoire now. It is an extremely spacious work, which unfolds lazily and deliberately. The first movement is introduced by five single notes on the tympani that act as a rhythmic motto for the entire work, constantly weaving in and out of the texture. The second movement is one of the longest and sweetest that Beethoven wrote, allowing the solo violin ample time to elaborate on its themes. A rondo finale in a six-eight hunting rhythm provides a joyful end to the work. Beethoven transcribed this concerto for piano, one of a very few pieces he adapted for other uses.

Overtures

Coriolanus, op. 62

Although Beethoven wrote only one opera, he did compose incidental music for several theatrical productions, among them an 1807 play based on the story of the Roman general Coriolanus. Banished from Rome, Coriolanus returns swearing to destroy the city. Only the fervent appeals of his wife and daughter stay his hand, and he is eventually executed for treason. Beethoven's overture to the play captures the drama of the situation clearly with its opening chords and heavy theme. A second theme represents the family's pleading, and the overture's sonata form beautifully represents the conflicting passions of the tale.

Leonora no. 3, op. 72a

The overture we now call *Leonora* no. 3 was the overture to the 1806 revival of *Fidelio*, later abandoned and replaced. Written at the height of Beethoven's heroic period, it is one of his greatest orchestral compositions. From its troubling introduction through its cantering first theme and graceful second theme to its shattering conclusion, the *Leonora* no. 3 is one of Beethoven's most overwhelming musical statements, almost an orchestral commentary on the action of the opera rather than an introduction to it. It was precisely the power of this overture that necessitated its removal. Anything coming after it would have sounded anticlimactic. Nonetheless, as a stand-alone concert piece, it is almost a textbook example of Beethoven at the height of his middle-period orchestral mastery.

Egmont, op. 84

Beethoven admired Goethe all his life, eventually meeting him in 1812, during the fateful summer of the Immortal Beloved. In 1810, Beethoven had contributed incidental music to a production of

Goethe's play *Egmont*, the overture to which is still performed. This curtain-raiser suffers some of the same faults as the *Leonora* no. 3: its drama is so complete that the play itself seems a letdown. The first theme of the *Egmont* Overture builds like the first theme of the *Leonora*, and the musical tension is maintained throughout the work.

Piano Sonatas

Sonata no. 8 in C Minor, op. 13 (*Pathétique*)

Beethoven first displayed his genius as a composer in his piano sonatas, and the *Pathétique* was his first great hit. Written a year or so before the First Symphony and the opus 18 string quartets, the *Pathétique* is musically more sophisticated than either later composition. From the opening introductory chords, the *Pathétique* proceeds with immense assurance. After a passionate first movement, the famous andante cantabile provides an idyllic resting place before a lighter finale completes the piece. The finale may let the work down a bit as it cannot maintain the level of power and beauty both earlier movements achieve. Nonetheless, the *Pathétique* remains one of Beethoven's most popular works, one of a handful of his first-period works that are still regularly performed.

Sonata no. 13 in C-sharp Minor, op. 27, no. 2 (*Moonlight*)

With its obsessively repeated rhythm, the first movement of the *Moonlight* Sonata is almost as well known as the first movement of the Fifth Symphony. Beethoven was experimenting with sonata form in this movement, attempting to create an introductory mood that would set up the climax of the final movement. This last movement is one of the stormiest Beethoven ever wrote but has little emotional connection to the first. Beethoven's desire to push the musical interest of his works nearer to their conclusion became a feature of his second-period style, but he learned to do so within the confines of traditional sonata form. Beethoven never repeated the experiment of the *Moonlight*, and its popularity eventually angered him, since he felt he had composed greater sonatas. It is still probably his most popular piano work.

Sonata no. 15 in D Major, op. 28 (*Pastoral*)

Composed just months after the *Moonlight*, the *Pastoral* Sonata bears the same relationship to its neighbor as the Sixth Symphony did to the Fifth. It is a peaceful, melodic counterpart to the storms of its predecessor. Beethoven, usually so laborious a composer, had less trouble with the *Pastoral* Sonata than with any other work he wrote. It just seemed to flow from his pen. The second-movement andante was one of Beethoven's favorites; he often played it for his own amusement.

Sonata no. 17 in D Minor, op. 31 no. 2

Only two of Beethoven's mature compositions are in the key of D minor: the Ninth Symphony and this sonata, one of a group of three composed in the fateful summer of 1802. Unlike the joyful Second Symphony, the mood of this sonata more closely approximates that expressed in the Heiligenstadt Testament, written just days after this work was completed. Beethoven employs many dramatic devices here, including a sort of solo recitative, which opens the work and returns in the recapitulation. (Consciously or not, Beethoven used this recitative again for the opening of the last movement of the Ninth.) The first movement is darkly tragic, the second formal and dignified and the third a kind of devil's dance, full of cross-accents and rolling arpeggios. Beethoven had commented to a friend that he was charting "a new path" with this work, which must refer more to the sonata's mood than to its relatively straightforward form.

Sonata no. 21 in C Major, op. 53 (*Waldstein*)

The *Waldstein* was Beethoven's first second-period sonata and is dedicated to the patron he had first known in Bonn. It is a work unlike any piano sonata Beethoven had previously composed, as original in its domain as the *Eroica* had been in its. Almost all the features we investigated in our analysis of the *Appassionata* Sonata are already present in this earlier work. The main theme of the first movement is more a rhythm than a melody, a series of rapidly repeated C-major chords that give the movement an irresistible forward motion. The movement is long: for the first time in a sonata the development section takes on added weight, and there is an extended coda as well. Beethoven discarded the second movement he had originally written for the *Waldstein* and replaced it with a sort of eerie bridge that looks ahead to both the Fourth Piano Concerto and the *Hammerklavier* Sonata. The final rondo is a technical minefield for all its rustic charm. A prestissimo final section brings this enormous work to a close.

Sonata no. 23 in F Minor, op. 57 (*Appassionata*)

See chapter 12.

Sonata no. 26 in E-flat Major (*Les Adieux*)

One of his rare sonatas from the waning years of the heroic decade, Beethoven dedicated this work to Archduke Rudolph and used Rudolph's 1809 flight from Vienna in the face of Napoleon's troops as a program for the work. The subtitle "Farewell, Absence and Return" explicitly refers to the Archduke's trials. However, apart from a melancholy slow introduction, which heartbreakingly expresses the "farewell" in the title, the work is in standard sonata form, with the second and third movements joined together. The first movement is spotty and nervous in keeping with the style Beethoven employed in the few pieces he wrote between his second and final periods. The second is a touching slow movement leading directly to a joyous third. Five years would pass before Beethoven again returned to the piano sonata.

Sonata no. 29 in B-flat Major, op. 106 (*Hammerklavier*)

The *Hammerklavier* is to the piano sonata what the Ninth is to the symphony: a massive, four-movement work that dwarfs every other composition in its field. Written in 1817–18, the *Hammerklavier* marks the beginning of Beethoven's late period. The enormous first movement shows remarkable unity: the entire four hundred bars are tied together by ideas whose harmonic relationship to each other is that of a falling third. The second-movement scherzo is based on the syncopated rhythm of its first two bars, spun out over several pages. The third-movement adagio sostenuto, marked "Passionately, with great sentiment," is the first of Beethoven's intense, almost religious late slow movements. (Ferrucio Bussoni, the noted twentieth-century pianist, refused his younger students permission to even sight-read this music, let alone learn it.) As if that weren't enough, a mysterious transition section opens up into the last movement, a full-scale, enormous fugue. Beethoven wrote several fugues as finales to his late works. Each is difficult both to play and to follow, the final movement of the *Hammerklavier* being no exception. After pages of intricate figuration, the sonata to end all sonatas comes to a close.

Sonata no. 32 in C Minor, op. 111

Beethoven did not maintain the scale of the *Hammerklavier* in the three sonatas that followed it. Instead, he retreated to the opposite pole, fashioning two-movement works of extreme compression. Such a work is this, his last sonata, written in 1822. The first of its two movements is a bizarre affair with melodic fragments spinning by as though tossed about by a strong musical wind. Even for the late Beethoven, this movement is terse and highly allusive. On the other hand, the second movement is almost immobile, a fifteen-minute theme and variations that never leaves the basic triads of C major. This "Arietta" is an ecstatic vision that becomes more excitable with each of its succeeding variations: at one point the music dissolves into nothing but a series of trills, twinkling points of musical light. As always with the late works, the most original musical effects are combined with a sure sense of craftsmanship that banishes any thought of artistic willfulness. Beethoven remained the master of his instrument from the formal reserve of op. 2, no. 1 to the spiritual abandon of op. 111.

String Quartets

Quartet op. 59, no. 1, in F Major (First *Razumovsky*)

In 1806, Beethoven turned his middle-period attention to the string quartet to satisfy a commission from Count Razumovsky, the Russian attaché in Vienna and one of the Austrian capital's most important patrons. As with the *Eroica* Symphony and the *Waldstein* Piano Sonata, the *Razumovsky* Quartets revolutionized their medium; no quartets of their caliber had appeared before. Op. 59, no. 1 was one of Beethoven's most controversial works, so full of confident innovation that many of its listeners were mystified. The first movement is very broad and spacious, with an opening theme that begins as though interrupted in the middle. The second-movement allegretto caused no end of astonishment when first heard, as its main theme is played on a single note. The quartet's original performers thought Beethoven was playing a joke on them with this movement. If the movement is a joke, it is a sublime one that creates a captivating mood with the slightest of means. A somber third-movement adagio leads directly to a finale based on a Russian theme, in honor of Razumovsky, that is one of Beethoven's most inspired. The work ends in high good humor.

Leaving many of his listeners behind, the *Razumovsky* no. 1 is indeed, as Beethoven remarked, a quartet "for the ages."

Quartet op. 59, no. 2, in E Minor (Second *Razumovsky*)

The second *Razumovsky* Quartet is in E minor, beginning immediately in a more dramatic vein than the first and conducting itself within a much narrower framework. Its exposition is one of the shortest written in Beethoven's middle period. The second-movement molto adagio was inspired by Beethoven's contemplation of the stars, reminding us of an entry Beethoven made in one of his Conversation Books many years later: "The starry heavens above us and the moral law within us: Kant!!!" Another Russian theme pops up during the minuet and trio, before a rousing finale returns us to E minor.

Quartet op. 59, no. 3, in C Major (Third *Razumovsky*)

The third op. 59 quartet is the most joyous of the three, despite the ominous tone of the slow introduction to its first movement and the minor key of its slow movement. Less expansive than the first, this third quartet makes up in melodic beauty what it may lack in structural complexity. The main theme of the first movement is a rushing figure that gives the opening its propulsion. The A-minor andante second movement has a theme that moves to major after a single phrase and then alternates from major to minor throughout the movement. An extremely old-fashioned minuet and trio follow like an unexpected visit from an elderly relative, before a fugal finale develops on a faintly comic opening motif. This hint of humor has wafted through the entire work, making us smile with pleasure in each movement.

Quartet op. 130 in B-flat Major

Op. 130 is Beethoven's *Hammerklavier* for the string quartet, a gargantuan multi-movement work that shattered the normal limitations of quartet form. Like the *Hammerklavier*, op. 130 was to end with a fugue movement, but even Beethoven realized that that was expecting too much of his audiences. The fugue movement was removed and published separately (as the *Grosse Fuge*), and Beethoven wrote a new finale. Although op. 130 was written in 1825, the added finale was the last composition Beethoven wrote before his death in 1827. Op. 130 is made up of six movements, which include some of the most interesting in Beethoven's repertoire. A first movement that switches tempi frequently is followed by a presto, which flashes by just quickly enough for us to enjoy its accelerated musical antics. The slow, third movement gives way to a little German dance, one of Beethoven's most charming miniatures, in which the original melody is split up between instruments and played both forward and backward. A second slow movement follows this march, in the tradition of the slow movement of the *Hammerklavier* and the "Holy Song of Thanks" of the A-minor late quartet. This songlike "Cavatina" had special significance for Beethoven, who admitted he could not even think of it without tears coming to his eyes. A simple melody in the first violin is played a few times before an extraordinary section marked "Afflicted" takes over, which sounds like a heart that keeps skipping a beat. Some have suggested that Beethoven rendered into music a slight stroke he may have suffered around this time. The opening melody returns to end this brief but moving interlude. Beethoven's friends were right in suggesting that a twenty-page fugue was not needed at this point in op. 130, and the new finale ends the piece on a much calmer and clearer note. Even with the new finale, however, op. 130 is one of the most demanding works Beethoven ever wrote.

Quartet op. 131 in C-sharp Minor

This seven-movement quartet is played without a break between movements, so it doesn't sound quite as experimental as it looks. Like op. 132, the language here is very truncated and terse. Musical ideas are just hinted at before abandoned. The first movement of the quartet is a fugue, and the heart of the work is a theme and variations, which is preceded by a sort of operatic aria for the first violin. Beethoven uses all the formal devices of his time in fashioning this work but still manages to stay within the confines of an elastic conception of sonata form.

Other Chamber Works

Septet op. 20

We are so familiar with Beethoven's grand compositions that we forget that he wrote his share of lighter, occasional music. Perhaps the most famous work in this vein was his op. 20 Septet, composed at the relatively late date of 1800. The Septet's six movements make few intellectual demands on listeners, charming them instead with a bounty of wonderful melodies. Beethoven eventually became frustrated by the extraordinary success of the Septet, feeling that his more serious work was being ignored by audiences content with a good melody and little else. The Septet became the model for works by many later composers, most notably Franz Schubert's Octet.

Violin Sonata op. 24 in F Major (*Spring*)

Beethoven wrote ten sonatas for violin and piano, all but two of them in his early period. Of these, the *Spring* Sonata is by far the most popular, due to its many infectious melodies. The opening violin line is one of Beethoven's most ingratiating themes, a line that bursts open like a spring bud. The second theme of the first movement is equally appealing, as are the short scherzo and the graceful finale. Beethoven's works have often been said to generally lack truly great melodies: the *Spring* Sonata shows Beethoven could turn quite a tune when he wished.

Violin Sonata op. 30, no. 3, in G Major

Beethoven wrote the three sonatas of opus 30 in 1802, and all demonstrate a growing confidence and maturity. The G Major Sonata starts energetically, slows for a second movement — which is more a minuet than an intense aria — and then takes off for a *perpetuum mobile* finale lasting a mere three and a half minutes. Throughout the work, but especially in its last movement, Beethoven's wit is paramount. Beethoven's humor is often hidden behind the serious mask he so often wore. Actually, few classical composers have peppered their work with more jokes and good fun. This sonata is one of Beethoven's most high-spirited.

Violin Sonata op. 47 in A Major (*Kreutzer*)

Only a few months separate the *Kreutzer* Sonata from op. 30, no. 3, but in that gap Beethoven's heroic style was born. The *Kreutzer* was composed in a hurry in the spring of 1803 (the soloist had to read his part from Beethoven's manuscript) just before Beethoven began work on the *Eroica*. Unlike any of its predecessors, it is written on a grand scale. It begins with a florid solo for the violin and continues for a first movement full of flourish and bravado. The middle movement is an enormous theme and variations that takes almost fifteen minutes to perform. Only in the final presto does the scale return more closely to chamber proportions, with a rollicking theme that stamps this ambitious work with generous good humor.

Trio op. 70, no. 1, in D Major (*Ghost*)

The piano trio — piano, violin and cello — was one of the most popular instrumental groupings of the late eighteenth century, allowing as it did for accessible amateur music making. All composers, including the greatest, were called upon to provide these kinds of at-home pieces. Beethoven's first published compositions — opus 1 — were three trios. After this youthful effort, Beethoven returned to the form twice for serious purposes and created some of his best chamber music. The *Geist* (Ghost) was one of three trios Beethoven wrote in 1808 that applied the heroic style to this older instrumental grouping. The trio's nickname comes from its mysterious second movement, adapted from a sketch Beethoven had made for an opera based on *Macbeth*, which never materialized. It is thus not ghosts but witches that are invoked in this movement. The atmospheric second movement is flanked by a strong, tightly focused first and a lively third.

Trio op. 97 in B-flat Major (*Archduke*)

The *Archduke* Trio, written in 1810–11 and named after Archduke Rudolph, to whom it was dedicated, was one of the last compositions Beethoven wrote during his second period and is a farewell to the heroic style. Each of its four movements is a model of perfection: all are presented in the majestic, calm style of a formal leave-taking. The piece begins with an elongated theme that serves as the basis for most of the movement's music. The development, especially, masterfully passes from an examination of one segment of the theme to the next, moving to the recapitulation when its developmental possibilities have been exhausted. The second-movement scherzo fully exploits the possibilities of this form, contrasting the dancelike minuet with a troubling minor-key trio. The third-movement theme and variations restores the majestic quality of the first movement and for the first time provides an extended coda to the last variation, tying this older form to the more modern sonata concept. A bouncy, headlong finale brings the work to a close. In the *Archduke*, the possibilities of the heroic style are just about exhausted. Beethoven had no choice after this work but to search out a new path. He would not find it for another five years.

Other Works

Thirty-three Variations on a Waltz by Diabelli, op. 120

In 1819, the Italian publisher and composer Antonio Diabelli asked fifty-one composers to each contribute a single variation on a piano waltz he had written, which would be included in a volume he was planning to publish. Beethoven at first refused the commission, then took two years to complete not one but thirty-three variations on Diabelli's modest little tune. Next to Bach's *Goldberg*, the *Diabelli* are the most extensive and complete set of variations ever written. The theme-and-variation format had always been very close to Beethoven's heart. Not only had he composed many sets for a variety of instruments, but variations also make up key movements in the *Appassionata* Sonata, the Third, Fifth and Seventh Symphonies, the *Kreutzer* Sonata and the *Archduke* Trio. In the *Diabelli*, however, Beethoven outdoes himself, turning the little waltz tune into a massive march, an atmospheric prelude, a section of *Don Giovanni* and everything else his fertile musical imagination could conjure up. At times the original theme is obviously present; at others it disappears into the deep background of a variation. After fifty-odd minutes of the most varied treatments, Beethoven relinquishes the exhausted theme, pushed and pulled by his genius beyond all recognition.

Mass in D Major, op. 123 (*Missa Solemnis*)

Beethoven's Grand Mass in D, the *Missa Solemnis*, was begun in 1819 for the installation of Archduke Rudolph as Bishop of Olmutz the following May. It wasn't completed until 1822. Beethoven had written to Rudolph: "There is nothing higher than to approach the Godhead more nearly than other mortals and by means of that contact to spread the rays of the Godhead through the human race" — a remarkable testament to the work's significance for its composer. Although based on the Latin text of the traditional Roman Mass, the *Missa*

Solemnis is a highly individual piece, full of word painting and extreme emotional tension. Beethoven felt a personal relationship to God the father, yet within his Mass was content to use the language that expresses the common humanity of all worshipers. Nonetheless, that the piece represents the religious sentiments of a single individual is never in doubt, which renders it less usable in a church setting, unlike the Masses of Bach. Each of the Mass's sections is unique and highly effective. A simple, warm *Kyrie* is followed by an explosive *Gloria*, which rings the heavens with its "Gloria in excelsis Deo." A convincing *Credo* follows (despite Beethoven's own lapsed Catholicism), before a hushed *Sanctus* celebrates the "Lord God of Hosts." Some commentators object to the excessive theatricality of the *Benedictus*, which features a lush solo violin interweaving with chorus and soloists, although there is universal praise for the dark *Agnus Dei* and the final *Dona nobis pacem*. The *Missa Solemnis* was composed just before the Ninth Symphony and there are many correspondences between the two works, one sacred, the other secular. Beethoven composed this work "from the heart," as he noted on the score, and it represents our closest approach to his religious sentiments and emotions.

Sources

Beethoven, Ludwig van. *Beethoven's Letters*. Edited by A.C. Kalisher. London: J.M. Dent, 1926. Reprint, New York: Dover Publications, 1972.

Cooper, Martin. *Beethoven: The Last Decade, 1817–1827*. Oxford: Oxford University Press, 1985.

Matthews, Denis. *Beethoven*. London: J.M. Dent and Sons, 1985.

Pestelli, Giorgio. *The Age of Mozart and Beethoven*. Cambridge: Cambridge University Press, 1984.

Ries, Ferdinand, and Franz Wegeler. *Remembering Beethoven*. Translated by Frederick Noonan. Berlin, 1906. Reprint, London: André Deutsch, 1987.

Rosen, Charles. *The Classical Style: Haydn, Beethoven, Mozart*. London: Faber and Faber, 1971.

Solomon, Maynard. *Beethoven*. New York: Schirmer, 1977.

Sullivan, J.W.N. *Beethoven: His Spiritual Development*. New York: Vintage Books, 1960.

Thayer, Alexander Wheelock. *Life of Beethoven*. Edited by Elliot Forbes. Princeton, NJ: Princeton University Press, 1967.

Index

The text of this book is set in Goudy, a graceful old style type
created by American designer Frederick Goudy in 1915.

Designed and typeset by James Ireland Design Inc.

Music settings by Michael Leibson